Will You Still
Love Me
If I Don't Win?

A GUIDE FOR PARENTS OF YOUNG ATHLETES

Will You Still Love Me If I Don't Win?

Christopher Andersonn

with Barbara Andersonn, MFCC

Taylor Publishing Company
Dallas, Texas

Designed by Janis Owens

Published by Taylor Publishing Company
1550 West Mockingbird Lane
Dallas, Texas 75235
www.taylorpub.com

Library of Congress Cataloging-in-Publication Data
Andersonn, Christopher.
Will you still love me if I don't win? : a guide for parents of young athletes/
Christopher Andersonn with Barbara Andersonn.
        p. cm.
Includes bibliographical references and index.
ISBN 0-87833-172-7
    1. Sports for children. 2. Parent and child. 3. Sports for children—
Psychological aspects. I. Andersonn, Barbara. II. Title.

GV709.2 .A53 2000
796'.083—dc21   99-056883

Printed in the United States of America

10 9 8 7 6 5 4 3 2 1

CONTENTS

Foreword

*W*ill You Still Love Me If I Don't Win? is one of the most powerful and important books you will ever read and experience. It will take courage to read this book and to apply what you will learn to your relationships with the people you love and cherish the most. Many self-help, psychology, or relationship books are written at a level that is far too shallow to make a difference. This book will affect you at a fundamental level that will make a difference in your life and the lives of your children. Every coach and every parent should read this book. I wish I could have read it thirty years ago.

I said it would take courage to read and experience this book. I speak from personal experience. I have been coaching for over thirty years and have known Chris Andersonn for twenty of those years. Chris has been working with my teams for most of the years I have known him. Every year, Chris would call me and ask if we were going to do the team seminar this year. Until two years ago, I would try to come up with some excuse as to why we might not be able to do it this year—timing, expense, etc. But the real reason was that I was nervous—no, scared—to commit to another seminar.

Why? I knew from previous seminars that Chris always helped our teams feel better about themselves as individuals, as athletes, and as teammates. In fact, it was always one of the most valuable experiences of the year, but still I was scared. The reason was that all of us, coaches and athletes, were encouraged through Chris's skillful and gentle guidance to become vulnerable with each other—and more importantly, with ourselves—and that scared me. Yet, during these sessions the athletes and coaches developed an intimate understanding of what was truly important in the athletic experience, and so little of it had to do with winning and losing. It had much more to do with our feelings and fears.

There are many who would say that my coaching career is almost perfect. I have coached Olympic Gold Medal winners, World Record holders, and 12 NCAA Team Championships, as well as many national champions and All-Americans. I have also been a United States Olympic coach for the past four Games—two as head coach—and I will serve once again as head coach for the 2000 Olympic Games in Sydney. It has been a dream come true to represent my country in international competition. It's been a dream career.

However, I have always felt there was much, much more to coaching and athletics than records and wins and losses. Most of the athletes I have coached are not Olympians or All-Americans, but all can have a winning and growing experience even if they never touch the wall first in a race. In fact, I have seen many great athletes—even Olympic gold medal winners—who had losing experiences in athletics.

Reading *Will You Still Love Me If I Don't Win?* and participating in the many seminars I have done with Chris have helped me to provide a safe place for our athletes to express their feelings and fears. They can do so without the additional fear that they will be judged as weak or labeled underachievers if they should fall short of their hopes and goals. Hopefully, my athletes realize they are loved and valued for who they are and not for what they do. I as a coach must always be asking myself if I am providing this safe place for them.

As a parent, I must always be asking myself if I am doing the same for my own children. This has become an everyday growing exercise for me. I never want my athletes or my children to feel they must "win" my love.

Ask yourself if your children must "win" your love. You as a parent are a very powerful force in the lives of your children, and I encourage you never to underestimate your impact on their lives. Chris Andersonn's book can be a very valuable tool that will challenge you to look at your relationship with your children and the role you play in what they feel and fear in their day-to-day lives and as athletes. Athletics is just the vehicle that Chris uses to illustrate a much deeper understanding of ourselves and our relationships.

The many stories that are told in the book are real life, and I found that each one caused me to evaluate myself and my feelings toward various situations and relationships I have had and currently have. I found that the differences between my personal experiences and those presented in the book have been in degrees, not kind. Reading them has been a growing experience not only as a coach but also as a parent.

This book will challenge you to evaluate what is important to you in your relationships and to help you to enhance them. Chris does an outstanding job of presenting many of the problems we all face as parents and giving us tools and methods to address these problems.

The challenge for all of us is to realize that there is no formula that fits all situations or all relationships, primarily because feelings and emotions play such an important role. *Will You Still Love Me If I Don't Win?* offers valuable insight, techniques, and suggestions as to how you can recreate yourself into a more understanding, caring, and loving parent.

A fear I have is that you might say, "I don't need this, my child knows I love him (or her)." I would say to you, "You are probably the one who needs the information in this book the most."

I wish the best of everything to those of you who accept the challenge of experiencing this powerful book. I am confident you will never regret using it as I have never regretted having Chris do the seminars with my teams. I know the athletes have benefited a great deal, but I am sure I have benefited the most.

Richard Quick
Women's Swimming Coach
Stanford University, Palo Alto, California

Preface

*W*hen *first asked* to read *Will You Still Love Me If I Don't Win?*, I did not appreciate what a guide to the parents of young athletes might offer the average parents. After all, Chris Andersonn's name was associated with top athletes, and only a very small percentage of the children I have seen as a child psychiatrist could be considered as such. As I read the manuscript, however, I came away with the impression that this book is not about athletes at all. It is a primer for how parents might handle themselves and their children irrespective of athletic endeavors. Chris captures through his experience the most important aspects of parenting gone awry and gives a point-by-point guide for change.

My experience over twenty years dealing with both seriously and not-so-seriously emotionally disturbed children has left me with many of the same concerns that Chris describes. The inability of a parent to truly separate his or her own needs from those of his child's is a fundamental problem for many children. When a child's performance is linked to the emotional well-being of the parent, it is a recipe for disaster. Chris, through the use of examples, makes this problem easy to see. Surely, parents reading this book will find ways in which they might be placing their own desires and feelings ahead of their child's. Impressively, this book offers examples from the author's real-life experiences that will resonate with all parents. Everyone will recognize the examples given, and hopefully, most will even recognize themselves in some.

The book is not simply a description of how parents often fail to truly meet their children's needs, however. It examines a number of possible hidden motivations which might lead a parent to unwittingly "miss the mark" with his child. Moreover, through the use of questions and exercises, a conscientious parent can find remedies without years of therapy!

In summary, this book is about good parenting. When we wonder rhetorically why mandatory reading is not required of prospective parents before having children, we are thinking of books such as this.

Robert Hines, M.D.
Child Psychiatrist
Former Medical Director of the Children's Psychiatric Unit at
St. Mary's Hospital in San Francisco, California, and Consultant
to St. Vincent's School for Boys in Marin County, California
Mill Valley, California

Acknowledgments

Writing this book has been an adventure in itself, spanning five years. I wanted to write something that would affect you emotionally, not just add to your intellectual store of information. It was important to present it in a way that would help you reflect, discover, and hopefully better understand your emotional role as a parent. I hope I have accomplished this.

Becoming more emotionally aware—and responsible—takes commitment and time. Yet, anything that has real value in our lives does take just that. In this case, the value you place on your emotional awareness will directly reflect upon your relationship with your children.

I want to thank the many parents with whom I have had countless conversations—in restaurants, cars, parking lots, seminar rooms, on telephones, and through letters—for inspiring and encouraging me to write this book. Some of them were uncommon examples of how to successfully raise children, demonstrating that work, family, school, and competitive athletics can all fit wonderfully well under one roof. And there were many who were desperate just to find a way to talk to their son or daughter. All of them were in my thoughts each night when I sat down and began to write.

Several people have contributed to the creation of this book. Barbara, my dear wife, has been my partner from the beginning. She has been my editor, reading—often several times— each page, making sure that what I wrote was clear and what I wanted to say. Her feedback and support throughout the writing of this book has been invaluable, and I am forever grateful. Peny and Michaell North have been inspirational to me in ways that have continually expanded my imagination and personal growth. Jach Pursel has been key to so much of what I have learned over the last twenty years. His contribution to my life cannot be measured in words. I thank Lazaris for his love, friendship, and guidance in helping me learn and grow beyond what I could ever have imagined. This book could not have been written without him. My friend Dick Schiendler has believed in me since the very beginning, when few others did, which has helped me in ways that I will be always grateful for. Richard Quick has offered me the opportunity to learn about coaching and young athletes in ways that have richly contributed to my life and my personal growth. He has also been a good friend. Not enough can be said about Fred Francis, my editor at Taylor Publishing. He has taken on this project from our first phone call, when I was a stranger to him looking for a publisher, to its completion as a finished book. His talents as an editor are brilliant and much appreciated.

Introduction

A coach once told me that he pictured the foundation of competitive sports like a three-legged stool. The first leg was technique, the physical skills of the sport. The second leg was psychology, which he defined as goal setting, positive thinking, mental preparation, and so forth. And the third leg was the actual training, or practice, of the sport. But after some years of coaching, he recognized that something was missing. There was a fourth leg on the stool, ultimately the most important. It was the emotional side of sports.

In my experience, this emotional side of sports—the way athletes feel about themselves and the effect those feelings have on their performance—is the most significant issue affecting young athletes today. There is no doubt that unresolved anger, pressure-producing fear, disappointment, hurt, and other suppressed feelings can handicap an athlete's abilities. At the very least, emotional pressure can turn competitive athletics into an emotional struggle, taking all the fun out of the sports experience. These problems are not about thinking, they are about feeling: emotions.

Yet, although there has been a lot of talk about the need to deal with the mind—the mental side of sports—rarely has there been much focus on the importance of dealing with the emotional side of sports. *Will You Still Love Me If I Don't Win?* not only discusses the effects of emotional stress on young athletes, it also explores the causes of that stress, including the integral role that you, the parent, play. But most importantly, you will find insight and practical techniques to help you and your children deal effectively with emotions and the situations that cause them. This book offers you valuable tools to create a more positive sports experience and a greater sense of well-being for your family.

My interest in the emotional stress on young athletes is long standing. My own years as a competitive athlete and my professional experience as a middle school and high school physical education teacher gave me the initial impetus to explore this virtually ignored aspect of the sports world. My ongoing journey of personal growth—including the study of psychology, philosophy, and spirituality—has nurtured and intensified my focus, leading to and expanding my work with young athletes and their parents. Consequently, during the past twenty years I have worked extensively with parents, coaches, and young athletes to develop a series of unique seminars, including the Hidden Athlete Seminar and the Parent's Seminar. This book is an outgrowth of all these experiences.

In looking back upon my own experience as a young athlete, I can still remember the tightness in my stomach and the weakness in my legs just before I competed in every basketball game or track meet. Sometimes it was the competitive juices flowing; other times I was just plain scared. I was so nervous before some basketball games that during warm-ups I had a difficult time controlling my energy. I jumped amazingly high, much higher than I usually could. It was the strangest feeling, like I had springs in my legs. But after ten minutes or so, after burning all that nervous energy, I would feel weak, almost as if I needed to sit down to regain my strength.

Yet, in fourteen years of athletic competition, I never spoke to anyone about my fears or, for that matter, any other emotions. As boys, and then young men, my friends and I never discussed our fears, disappointments, or anxieties—no one did, certainly not our coaches. We talked about girls and winning basketball games and how good or bad we played on a given day—serious, male kinds of things, or at least we thought so. Besides, I was afraid it was weak to ever admit to my fear. When I did feel anxious before a game, I just tried to act confident, hoping no one would notice.

It was in my mid-teens that I first began to hear people talk about "positive thinking." To me that meant not thinking negative thoughts. I did not yet understand that thinking came from my intellect and feeling came from my emotions, and that they were significantly different from each other. I just lumped thoughts and feelings all together. And since I thought fear equaled weakness, and therefore was a "negative thought," I tried my best to suppress even further any feelings of fear. I did not see until much later in my life that I was giving myself less and less permission to feel any emotions. I lumped anger, hurt, disappointment, despair, etc., all together as "negative thoughts," which I thought—if I was a strong person, a real athlete—I had to suppress. Unfortunately, this only served to bury my feelings deeper, in turn causing even more emotional pressure whenever I competed.

In looking back, I now know that the emotional pressure I continually felt prevented me from achieving my fullest potential as an athlete. More significantly, the pressure exacted a toll on my sense of personal value, self-worth, and overall well-being. I felt as if I always had to fake who I was and what I was feeling, hoping no one saw anything less than the confident, in-control athlete. Without a way to understand or deal with my feelings, I became a prisoner of them. Outwardly, I may have appeared confident, but inwardly I was always scared of what everyone thought of me.

It was not until my mid-thirties that I finally began to understand that fear, anger, and disappointment—as with all emotions—are meant to be felt, not suppressed. And it is healthy and emotionally—as well as physically—freeing to feel emotions. It is not a sign of weakness, as I so strongly believed as a young athlete.

Today's young athletes are no more comfortable dealing with their emotions than I was, and they face even greater pressures. There are more sports, more athletes—particularly girls—more leagues, more teams, more competitions, and more participating parents than ever before. This has led to more college scholarships, more television and print media coverage, more pro athletes, more athletic shoe and apparel companies, and ultimately, more money being spent in the world of sports. The combination of all of these things has placed a tremendous focus on performance and winning. And young athletes most certainly feel the pressure of that focus.

In the athlete's seminars I conduct it is common to see children, teens, and even college athletes break into tears when they speak of their fear of failing their parents, coaches, teammates, and themselves. Even if they are very successful in their sport, most feel the continual emotional pressure of having to live up to their own success.

Young athletes are fundamentally children and adolescents in the process of growing up, trying to discover who they are. They are not experienced professionals with athletics as their only focus in life. They are young people struggling to deal with their emotional ups and downs in today's highly competitive athletic atmosphere.

Fortunately, a growing number of concerned coaches and parents are very aware of the emotional stresses that young athletes face. However, concern and awareness are only the beginning steps to dealing with the problem. The difficulty is in knowing what to do, how to help.

Raising a competitive athlete is, without a doubt, an emotional challenge. The reason for creating the Parent's Seminar was to help the parents of young athletes meet that challenge. In seminars across the country, I have shared with parents the types of emotional pressures their kids face. They have shared with me the problems and conflicts they face. Our discussions have explored just about every problem and potential solution young athletes encounter. And during this process, parents have opened up and, often for the first time, have recognized how important it is to deal more effectively with their own feelings, not just help their children deal with theirs. Wonderful changes have happened in families as a result.

Similarly, the Hidden Athlete Seminar was developed to provide an opportunity for young athletes to remember that they are people first—with feelings—not just "athletes" as they so often see themselves.

What is a Hidden Athlete? Simply put, there is a free and budding athlete inside of every young competitor, yet that athlete can become "hidden," lost under the weight of suppressed emotions—particularly fear. When the weight of those emotions is removed or even lightened, the part of that athlete that became hidden can rise to the surface.

The experience of doing the Hidden Athlete Seminars was one of the motivations for writing this book. It was apparent, again and again, just how much fear exists in competitive sports for our youth, regardless of their level of talent. This is based primarily on a fear of "loss of love" if they do not perform well enough. Losing their parent's love—even though they may be very loved—is their greatest fear, but they also fear losing approval, acceptance, and acknowledgment—all forms of love—from coaches, friends, teammates, and, in some cases, the general public.

The phrase "loss of love" is sometimes difficult to accept for many parents, who say, "My son knows I love him." Yes, this is generally true, but when that son was an infant and young child—from birth to five years of age particularly—his entire sense of security was threatened if he sensed any disappointment or rejection from his parents. This exists in all infants and children, and it is still very much a part of their subconscious when they grow older. It is this fear that can so quickly surface when there is the risk of failing or disappointing a parent—or anyone else—even if that child knows he is loved.

Unfortunately, for some children and teens the fear of losing love is a day-to-day experience. A significant percentage of young athletes feel continually pressured by their parents. In talking to many of these parents, few, it seems, rarely consider their actions as anything less than totally loving. The truth is, some of their actions are not loving or supportive at all. They easily forget that subtle actions—looks, repeated phrases, tones of voice, the withdrawal of attention—carry significant messages.

On the other hand, most parents are genuinely supportive and loving and are willing to do whatever they can to be better parents. This does not mean their children feel unconcerned about how their performance will be perceived. Because children base their concepts of love on how their parents relate to them, and no parent can ever love perfectly, the fear of losing a parent's love, to varying degrees, is a natural condition in every child.

This book is meant to help you look at your relationship with your children. And, as at any time you look at your life, you must first begin with open and honest self-reflection. This takes courage, for you run the risk of seeing something you may not like about yourself. Or you may be reminded of experiences and emotions long ago suppressed. You may be surprised at how similar some of your son's or daughter's issues are to your own issues. If you do, good. It will help you have an even deeper understanding of those issues and a greater sense of empathy for your son or daughter.

Above all, this book is about loving, about young people and their needs (whether they are athletes or not), and about you and your needs. And it is about the ever-growing and expanding relationship between you and your children.

There is pain and disappointment as well as joy, celebration, and happiness in every family, particularly in a young athlete's family where competition is such a part of life. Love is what mends the pain and soothes the disappointment. Love is what allows for the laughter and the compassion. And being loved is what every child wants to be reassured of the most.

My intent is that this book be both a guide and a catalyst for you, not an encyclopedia of information. Many things cannot be learned through logic and explanation. They have to be discovered and felt. My hope is to present my experience and advice in a way that will give you useful information, as well as help you discover, perceive, and feel what is being said between the lines.

Throughout the book there are suggested approaches to handling specific problems that you face as a parent. At the same time, there are no lists or summaries at the end of each chapter. This is to avoid encouraging parents to "do this," and "then this," and "then this," or to believe that a series of simple steps are the point of this book. That can easily end up becoming a shallow and simplistic approach to addressing complex and often long-standing emotional issues.

Perhaps most of all, this book is about helping you increase your emotional awareness. Such awareness is essential in leading you to a deeper understanding of how to expand and express your love and support for your children.

My fondest desire is to help you and your young athlete(s) find more enjoyment, success, and peace, as well as to help your children build a solid foundation for a fulfilling life through a healthier sports experience.

Having said all this, the introduction would not be complete if I were not to share with you perhaps the most important reason this book has been written. That reason began when I was seven years old.

After my parents had separated, my mother ended up raising both me and my older sister, Jill. Jill, an outstanding athlete, always looked out for me, and when I was seven, she began teaching me how to play sports. The one I liked the most was kickball, so she made sure I was included in her morning kickball games, even though I was by far the youngest—and the only boy.

It was during one of these early morning games that everything changed for me. Jill had been teaching me how to kick a ball, because on my own I was having all sorts of trouble, sending kicks everywhere. It took several days and a lot of patience and encouragement, but it paid off.

During a particular game on a cool, foggy San Francisco morning, with my jacket zipped up to my neck to keep me warm, I stepped up to the plate and walloped the heck out of the ball, sending it careening into center field. It was the first time I had ever really kicked a ball well. I was so stunned at what I had done that I just stood there with my mouth open and watched the ball as it flew through the air. Then I heard the cheering and the excitement, and at everyone's yelling and urging, I ran for my life for first base.

Suddenly I was the center of attention. Everyone was laughing and happy. It was a powerful and exciting feeling that ended up changing my future. From that day on, sports became both my haven and my obsession.

During the next few years my father, whom I rarely saw, sort of faded out of my life. My mother began drinking more and more heavily, finding her own way of disappearing. Jill still watched out for me, but she had begun spending more time away from home with friends her own age. I found myself spending my afternoons and weekends at South Sunset playground, and after homework and dinner, I went to the local gym each week night and played basketball until closing time.

By the time I was twelve, my family had become the guys at the gym, and I was captivated by the game of basketball. Basketball was going to be my path to becoming someone, I decided. And I was going to earn an athletic college scholarship—as a basketball player. Just hearing the sound of it— "a basketball player"—made me feel good about myself. I had found an identity I could hold onto, and a dream I could hope for.

As it turned out, basketball was indeed my sport. I was talented and constantly improved until it looked like I might actually reach my goal. When I was seventeen, a senior in high school, my team was ranked number one in Northern California. We were good. Things were on track for an outstanding year.

Then the strangest thing happened.

During a game in the annual Christmas tournament, I began having trouble running up and down the court for more than a few minutes without feeling completely out of breath. My coach yelled at me for being out of condition and took me out of the game. I was put back in a little later, but my condition seemed even worse. I just could not get enough air inside of my lungs to be able to breathe, let alone keep up with the guy I was supposed to guard. My coach took me out again, this time for good. As it turned out, that was the last high school basketball game I ever played in.

I found out that something was wrong with the sac surrounding my heart, as well as with my lungs. A week later, my left leg swelled overnight to almost twice its size. A major blood clot had developed in my left leg.

Ironically, as I waited for the ambulance that was coming to take me to the hospital, the phone rang. To my utter shock, it was the basketball coach from a university. He asked me how I was doing—he had just talked to my coach. I apologized for my shaky voice and said not so good, that I could not talk very long—I was having trouble standing. He apologized for calling me, wished me a good recovery, and then offered me an athletic scholarship. I was speechless, overjoyed, and in too much pain to know what to say. So I just said thank you and asked if I could call him back.

As it turned out, the blood clot in my leg caused a permanent blockage of the deep vein, prohibiting normal blood flow. My circulation system could not stand up to the rigors of basketball, no matter how hard I tried to convince myself otherwise.

When I finally called the coach and told him I could not accept the scholarship, it felt like a part of me died.

Being an athlete had been my identity since the age of seven. If I could not be an athlete, who would I be? How could I be worth anything? I had no idea, and it scared me. And to lose basketball—to lose my dream? That did not seem possible; it was my life. I felt like I was nothing without it—a black hole, existing nowhere, doomed to disappear altogether.

These thoughts were not true, of course. My self-worth and identity were not linked to whether I was an athlete, but I did not even begin discovering that until my mid-thirties. Until then, I believed that my real future had been lost.

Of course a lot of self-pity and pain were mixed up with my feelings, not to mention a few somewhat twisted adolescent ideas about life. But as long as they were in place, I was trapped by them—and always felt like I had missed the boat.

Eventually, through a journey of personal growth, everything changed. A process of healing led me to discover that everyone is worthwhile, lovable, and valuable just as we are, successful athletes or not. And this recognition, more than anything else, is what led me to want to work with young people—young athletes—so I might be able to help them see what I could not see at their age.

When I first began talking with young athletes, it seemed that everywhere I looked was a younger version of me. So many were doing just what I had done, linking up their value and self-worth to their success as athletes.

Many spoke to me—in seminars, in private conversation, in letters, and on the phone—about their anguish, their sense of being failures. They feared not being able to live up to their success, feeling left out and disappointing their parents.

Many also spoke to me about their love of the sport, their friends, the great joy of winning, and how wonderful it was to be a part of their team. And when they had to leave the team, or when they were graduating from school and moving on in their lives, they cried at the sweet memories and for the friends they knew they would miss.

It has been, and continues to be, a wonderful experience to be with them, to see them support each other and to listen to them open up emotionally for the first time in their lives, and to watch them discover, and be moved by, how many of their teammates care about them. They laugh and they cry. They ask questions and talk to each other about what they are feeling. They learn that they can be open and honest. They see deeper parts of themselves, and each other, for the first time. And they learn that competing in sports is about so much more than just their performance.

What is the purpose of this book? Perhaps in its simplest form, it is to help you make it easier for your children, who are young, impressionable, and prone to making snap judgments about themselves, to learn that they do not have to do or be something to be loved. They are lovable and worthwhile just as they are. And that worthwhile part of them can never be lost. It is not something they can earn or lose. It is God-given, and it is with them every moment of their lives.

Young Athletes

CHAPTER 1

It's Scary to Be a Young Athlete

O*ne hot, muggy summer,* I traveled to the Midwest to conduct a seminar on the mental and emotional side of sports with a swimming team. During a break, I saw a little boy about eight years old, in his swimming suit, run into one of the stalls in the boys' bathroom and throw up. Concerned, I asked if he was all right. "Yes," he mumbled, just before he ran out of the stall and back out onto the pool deck.

A few minutes later, when I returned to the pool deck, the coach I was working with approached me and asked if I would mind talking to one of his younger swimmers. It was the young boy I had seen in the bathroom.

"He throws up before every meet he competes in, and he'd like to know why that is," the coach said. "I told him you might be able to help him."

"I can try," I said, turning to the boy. After a few minutes of conversation about swimming and his particular events, I asked, "Are you a pretty good swimmer?"

"I guess so . . . I don't know," he replied.

"Are your parents very interested in your swimming?"

"My dad is."

I looked around and spotted a man sitting in the bleachers staring at us intently. "Is that your dad over there? The one with the two stopwatches hanging around his neck and the clipboard on his lap?"

"Yes! How did you know?" he asked, wide-eyed.

"Oh, just a lucky guess," I replied.

I asked if his dad attended all his practices. Yes, he did the boy answered.

I asked him if he was concerned that his dad might be disappointed in him if he didn't do well. He thought so. Then I asked if he thought his dad might stop loving him if he didn't continue to improve.

He looked at me for the longest time, then finally lowered his eyes and said in a very soft voice, "I don't know."

"It must be very scary not knowing if your dad will still love you if you don't swim fast enough," I said gently, "perhaps scary enough to make you feel so much pressure that you feel sick to your stomach before every big race." He continued staring at the ground, not moving, not saying a word.

"Would you be willing to go over and ask your dad something? Ask him if he will still love you if you don't swim fast enough. Tell him I wanted you to ask this question because you don't know the answer."

He looked up at me, hesitating, and I asked, "Can you do it? I know it takes a lot of courage. I can go with you if you like."

"That's okay . . . I can do it by myself," he answered. I told him I would be right there if he needed me, and then watched him walk over to his father to ask the question.

The father, who had been watching us while we were speaking, now looked at his slowly approaching son. I was too far away to hear their conversation, but I could easily see the boy, with his head down, ask the question. As his father listened, his face went from stunned surprise to sadness. He glanced at me, then turned back to his son, put his clipboard and pen aside, reached out, and just held him.

There are many fathers (and mothers) who participate in their children's sports to this degree without ever realizing the impact they are having on their children. This father, like many others, became so focused on his son's performance that he failed to even notice how terrified his son had become of disappointing him—to the point of regularly becoming physically sick to his stomach. This is not an example of a father just being supportive and interested in his child's sport. It is an excessive form of parental control, and it produces fear and insecurity in children. How much fear would it take for this son to completely rebel and drop out of sports forever, for fear he could never live up to his father's expectations? Or would there come a time when the amount of pent-up fear became so great that it would cripple the son's confidence and potential in everything he attempted to do in his life? All too often, this latter scenario is a common outcome of a father-son relationship like the one described.

This story, which was written for *Swimming World and Junior Swimmer* in April 1995, speaks clearly of the fear that so many young athletes experience. It exemplifies the lack of emotional awareness and sensitivity that so many parents demonstrate.

I speak to young athletes from different countries, from various cultures, and from all parts of America. Though there is a multitude of differences among them—sex, size, strength, age, ability, and so forth—they all share common ground. This has nothing to do with the kind of sport they participate in, or for that matter that they all happen to be athletes. All of them share one significant thing in common—their emotions—and for the vast majority, fear is the one emotion they talk about most.

Yet, many parents are not aware of their children's fear, or how much they themselves affect it. The key for parents in becoming more aware lies in understanding why their children are afraid.

Perhaps the first thing to understand is that young athletes do not normally experience constant fear. Rather, their fear comes and goes, depending upon several variables—their age, their level of failure and success, the expectations laid upon them by themselves and others, divorce, sibling rivalry, and family problems.

Many of their fears are similar, whether boy or girl, American or Australian, young or old. They fear being very successful—then they have to live up to it. They fear failing—that could be humiliating. They fear beating their friends—that might threaten their friendships. They fear disappointing their parents, coach, and teammates—that brings up fear of rejection or judgment. Fear, in one form or another, for the majority of young athletes is very much a part of their world.

It is important to understand that fear is not something young athletes should try to eliminate—that is not possible. It is human to experience fear—particularly in competitive situations. Rather, the idea is that they can learn how to manage their fear more effectively.

Some parents, trying to understand an athlete's fear, have asked the question, "Surely the best athletes, the ones who regularly succeed, are much more confident than average athletes. After all, they are the winners. Don't they feel less stress?" Logically it might seem that winners should feel more confidence and less stress, but winners face a significant problem. They are always at risk of losing what they have achieved—their "mystique," their status of being the best, their sense of personal power. You would be surprised how many star athletes, from the tender age of ten and eleven to well into their twenties, break into tears when they talk about their fears of failing and being humiliated and rejected—particularly by their coaches or parents:

A 14-year-old girl named Maria approached me after a seminar, agitated and seemingly terrified of anyone hearing our conversation. "Can we talk in private?" she asked.

We went to the coach's office.

"I was one of the best in the country when I was ten," she began, "I won everything. My parents were so happy. I was going to the Olympics, everyone said. My parents even talked about which year I would probably make the team and began planning their trip to be with me."

She then covered her face with her hands and burst into tears.

"What happened?" I asked.

"I don't know," she answered. "I just began gaining weight when I turned twelve. I got bigger and bigger—I couldn't stop it! I'm thirty pounds overweight now. Too fat to compete like I used to. My parents have put me on ten different diets—none worked. I have lost all my rankings. I'm having trouble just staying on the team. What am I going to do? I don't know what to do. I'm a total failure."

She was staring at her shoes and wringing her hands while she spoke. Her face and neck were flushed. She suddenly blurted out, "I've started putting my finger down my throat after meals so I could throw up my food."

She looked up at me. "I'm scared. What if my parents find out? I can't disappoint them again."

"Am I the only person who knows you are throwing up?" I asked.

"Yes," she answered.

"This is too big a burden for you to carry all by yourself. You need to talk to your parents about this. Give them the opportunity to help you—to love you. You can't do this by yourself anymore," I told her. "You are so afraid to disappoint them again. I understand that. But how do you think they would feel if they knew you would not even ask for their help when you really needed it?"

She did not answer.

"Do you really want to continue hating yourself and feeling all alone in the world?" I asked.

"No."

"Who is the easiest for you to talk to? Your mom or dad?" I asked.

"Mom," she answered.

"Go home and tell her everything. Tell her how bad you feel about disappointing her. And tell her what you are doing as an attempt to lose weight. Don't hold back anything. Give her the chance to love you."

After a few minutes, she said okay, she would talk to her mother.

That night Maria and her mom and dad met with me. She had indeed talked to her mother. It was amazing. She was a different person—laughing, relaxed, spontaneous, as if fifty pounds had been lifted off her back. Her parents, on the other hand, were subdued, shaken, attentive.

Maria began. "I never realized how much pressure I put on myself to live up to all the success I had at ten. Everyone was talking about what was going to happen when I got older—nationals, then the Olympics. My coach was excited. He believed in me. My parents were talking about which Olympics I would be in so they could come and watch me. Even I was confident and excited about my future. Then one day—I don't even know why—I started thinking, "What if I failed? What if for some reason I lost my talent, or others passed me by, or it just turned out that I wasn't really that good anymore? I started to get scared. I would disappoint so many people. Just thinking about it made me even more scared. I never had doubted myself until then. And then all at once, it seemed like everything began going downhill from there."

Her father added, "I never realized how much pressure I was putting on her."

Her coach joined us after awhile, and we continued talking. The coach said he knew all along what the weight was about. It was fairly common to see an athlete become very successful at a young age and then end up not being able to deal with the pressure of having to live up to it. He said that on several occasions he had brought up to the girl the subject of how much pressure she might be feeling. He had wanted to give her a chance to talk about it, hoping he could open the door for her. She just closed down, not wanting to go anywhere near the subject. He had talked to the parents early on about his concerns for her. Their answer was to find another diet.

When we began, the mother looked almost as bad as the girl had looked earlier in the day, but she became stronger as the evening went on. She told her daughter repeatedly, "It's okay; we'll work this out. We are here for you, whether you ever compete again or not. We love you."

The father was quiet, except when he was reassuring and apologizing to his daughter.

The girl beamed, basking in her parents' attention.

The stress of living up to inordinate success is only one way fear can eat away at and break down a young athlete's confidence.

Another way is unexpected failure.

Many athletes, particularly young ones, never achieve at a high level again after experiencing a devastating loss. They are simply too frightened to face the deep pain of disappointment, shame, and humiliation ever again.

He was only fifteen, yet he looked older. His body was muscular and powerful looking. Throughout the seminar he had been sitting in the back of the room, observing quietly. When he raised his hand and I called on him, the room became very attentive. All eyes were on him, expectant.

"I don't know how to begin . . ." he said, tears welling up in his eyes. "I was so good in this one event. I nearly always won whenever I competed in it. The state championships were coming up—it was two years ago—and I truly believed I was going to win."

Several of his teammates began tearing up. As it turned out, they had been at the same championships with him.

"I never saw it coming," he said. " I lost. Badly." He began to hyperventilate and cry at the same time. Through his tears, he choked out, "It was so humiliating!"

After a few minutes, he continued. "I have never been able to compete in that event since that day. I just can't do it—thinking about it is enough to make my whole body tighten up. It's like I can never get over it."

"You never did get over it," I said. "The pain of that loss is with you every day, every waking hour, lurking in the background, ready to come up and show itself. Though it is terribly painful and robs you of your confidence, it is there for a positive reason. It is your way of telling yourself that you need to heal it," I added. "It is trying to find a way out. You can get over it, but not unless you are willing to feel all that pain that is locked inside of you, the pain that comes up every time you think of that one race. If you can do that, you can heal it and move on. It will not guarantee that you can compete in that event like you did before, but you can regain that part of you that was lost."

"How do I do that. I can't live with this anymore," he said, through his tears.

"You have to go back in your imagination and feel what you felt that day—until it is gone," I answered. "Are you willing to do that? We can do it right now, right here. I'll take you through it. They won't mind," I said, looking around at the other athletes in the room. "They will be with you all the way."

After a pause, he said, "Okay. I want to do it."

I asked him to close his eyes and go back to that moment, two years ago, when he lost and felt so humiliated.

"Visualize the entire scene—in detail—all over again. This time let yourself feel every emotion that comes up—humiliation, embarrassment, pain, fear, sadness, anger, whatever. Don't hold back, and do not stop feeling until everything is gone," I told him.

"Take as much time as you need. We are in no hurry. Everyone here wants you to heal this," I added.

He closed his eyes and in a less than a minute everything came tumbling out. His entire body was shaking with pain and tears. No one in the room moved or spoke. They stayed with him, supporting him.

After fifteen minutes or so, he began to quiet down, his body gradually stopping its shaking, his breathing slowly coming back to normal. When he opened his eyes, he just looked down for awhile, saying nothing. His shoulders were hunched, his face red and tear-stained. When he finally looked up at me, he just held my gaze.

"I feel a whole lot better," he said. He looked around the room, and then added, "I want to thank all of you for taking the time to listen to me. I really needed this."

For some of you reading this, it might seem that youth sports could be an emotional roller coaster that is not worth the ride. That is not necessarily true, yet since emotions are such a major and often confusing part of any youngster's life, they simply cannot be ignored without consequence. That is why parents, coaches, and others associated with young athletes need to pay attention to how the athletes are feeling, for those feelings ultimately play a large role in shaping how they determine their sense of worth, value, and self-esteem.

Benefits and Drawbacks of Youth Sports

Ideally, youth sports will benefit the children and adolescents who participate in them, mentally, physically, *and* emotionally. That, hopefully, is the idea. If coaches and parents are balanced in their approach to the teaching, training, and support they offer, there will be benefits, some potentially great ones. If they are not balanced in their approach, there will be drawbacks.

The benefits and drawbacks listed here are meant to give you a general sense of the more common ones. Later in the book there is another, more detailed section on the potential benefits and drawbacks specific to the very demanding sports such as swimming and gymnastics. These sports are unique in youth athletics, offering a more intense and in-depth experience for those involved. They also carry their own distinct kind of benefits and drawbacks.

Perhaps the most obvious benefit is that youth sports gives children and adolescents the opportunity to challenge themselves, to see what they can learn and discover about themselves. The very challenge of it and the years of opportunity that are available to pursue the challenge can be great fun.

Just as valuable are all the friendships formed along the way. Having teammates and competitors to face teaches young athletes how to get along and how to respect others. It gives kids a chance to practice having relationships outside of normal school situations.

Competition gives young athletes the opportunity to face winning and losing, personally and as part of a team. This allows them to learn how to deal with the ups and downs of their feelings, which can sometimes be extreme. Facing competition also offers the chance for them to learn how to set goals, and how to work toward achieving them.

Youth sports can be an environment where another adult, the young athletes' coach or coaches, can positively influence them with encouragement, guidance, and care, often reaching them in areas of their lives where even their parents cannot.

And a big reason why youth sports can be beneficial is that being involved in sports after school is a lot more productive than hanging around the malls and street corners. Young athletes can gain a sense of purpose, self-esteem, and value that is not available to kids who lack direction and guidance. Young people involved with sports feel like they belong to something, which is so vital to them at their stage in life.

Though there are wonderful benefits to be gained through participating in youth sports, there can also be definite drawbacks. Some are obvious, while others cannot be seen until one is already involved in the sport.

One drawback can be the time commitment and financial burden youth sports often demand. Certain sports—swimming, ice skating, gymnastics—can demand much more time than others. This time crunch can put a strain on families, especially when sisters or brothers in the same family are not involved in sports. The parents' attention can be centered around the "athlete" to the exclusion of the "nonathlete."

And even if the entire family is into athletics, another drawback that can surface in the often-hectic life of a young athlete can be the lack of time the family has to spend with each other. All the traveling, training, and competing—on top of normal school responsibilities—leave little time for family socializing or trips. Some parents, after years of being involved in sports, have regretted this loss of time together with their children.

Coaches who are too controlling, too competitive, and too much in need of success put enormous pressure upon their athletes, often humiliating and scaring them. Many young athletes are emotionally damaged by such coaches. These coaches are notorious in all sports, and sadly are allowed to continue—and are even sought out by many parents who will do anything to help their child win.

Finally, young athletes may become involved in an unbalanced program, where all the emphasis is put upon winning. In such a program, nothing is done to help an athlete learn about his or her emotional self. In fact, for the most part fear and similar feelings are usually considered weak, and it is the athlete's job to figure out how to deal with them. There is no consideration to any kind of balanced development for the athlete. It is all about winning, which gives young people the message that their worth and value is determined by how well they perform. This is the wrong message for any child to receive.

This last drawback speaks to the lack of emotional development in competitive sports programs, and specifically to the way fear is usually looked upon by many coaches (and parents) and eventually by the athletes themselves. Ultimately, this approach will severely curtail or eliminate any real opportunity for young athletes to gain an awareness of how to deal with their emotions.

Where Is the Emotional Training for Young Athletes?

It might seem to follow that since fear is such a major aspect of competitive sports for young athletes, learning how to deal with it would naturally be a part of their training. Yet, in reality it is not. In fact, very little time, if any, is ever spent on a young athlete's emotional education.

Of the hundreds of coaches I have met, only a few know enough about dealing with their own emotions to feel comfortable teaching their athletes how to respond to their feelings. A coach's emphasis is predominantly on physical training, so taking time for emotional education is usually considered taking time away from what they consider to be the "real" training of athletes.

And, though many parents try their best to help their children, as with coaches, only a small percentage of them have the emotional awareness and skills to know what to do or say. Typically, children and teens are left to figure out how to deal with their emotions on their own, and when advice is given, it is usually in terms of, "Things will get better," "Think positive," "Try your hardest," "There is always another day," or "You did your best." These are all supportive suggestions, but none of them helps anyone deal with their fear—or any other complicated emotions they are feeling.

What young people are facing in competitive sports is an emotional dilemma. They are continuously confronted with stressful, emotional situations, particularly ones that produce fear. But because they have little or no emotional education, they have no way of effectively dealing with what they are feeling.

The Need for Change

Unless we adults change something—like how we view sports and what is really important in the lives of our young people—our young athletes will face a lack of overall development as people, particularly emotionally. We are setting them up to face life without a solid foundation they can rely upon. We need to offer more guidance and support. A good place to start is to create a new foundation for how we develop our young athletes, taking into consideration all aspects of who they are as people—particularly their emotions.

Many programs in competitive sports claim to offer just this, a balanced program of youth development. In reality, there are very few. All you have to do is look at what coaches spend their time focusing on, and you will know what they consider to be important. How much time do coaches spend on the physical? And how much time do they spend on other things, like helping young athletes learn about their emotions?

To be fair, not all coaches or organizations are able to—or even want to—run a truly balanced program, for reasons of lack of interest or ability, lack of knowledge, or budget and time constraints. And it is not just their responsibility. Ultimately, those who have the most influence, the most responsibility, and the most power over young athletes are the parents.

It is an awesome and daunting responsibility to raise a child, and to know that everything you say and do affects them—and their future. It can be even more complicated when your child is a young athlete. What is the best way to be supportive? When is the best time to talk to them after a big loss? And what is the right thing to say?

Hopefully, this book will give you a fair amount of help and guidance, at least in the area of competitive sports. However, you will see it really has to do with the dynamic of the parent-child relationship—whether your kids are athletes or not.

CHAPTER 2

The Key to Success: Developing the Whole Self

*T*he term success *in regard to* young athletes refers to something greater than being the one who wins the most competitions. True success for young athletes lies in how much they are able to develop all components of themselves as young people. This certainly includes achievement in the form of winning, but it does not focus solely on it. Other achievements, such as developing determination, becoming a supportive teammate, learning—and practicing— the skills of the sport, making new friends, etc., are all part of this greater concept of success. Added together, these achievements are invaluable to young people in their process of growing up—and in becoming successful athletes.

For young athletes to be able to develop all components of themselves, which collectively can be referred to as the "Whole Self," they must be given both opportunity and guidance. Most athletic programs focus predominantly on one component—the physical. While it is obviously a major part of sports, the physical is only one component of a young athlete's Whole Self.

When all components of the Whole Self are supported and nurtured, young people can gain greater balance and harmony in their lives. The synergy that is generated from this balance and harmony gives them a much better opportunity to achieve their fullest potential as athletes. Developing all components of the Whole Self, therefore, becomes the "key" to the kind of athletes—and people—they eventually will become.

Here is an example of how a young athlete can be affected when she is out of balance in the development of her Whole Self:

During one particular athlete's seminar, I asked everyone in the room to share with each other, one on one, the pressures they were feeling in their lives at that time. As they began talking to each other, I noticed one girl saying nothing to her partner. Her head was down and she was crying softly. Her partner tried to talk to her, but she continued crying. He finally gave up and just sat quietly with her. Ten or fifteen minutes later, when it was time for individuals to share with the entire group about their particular pressures, the girl who was crying was the first to raise her hand. Everyone in the room gasped. As I learned later, no one could remember her ever raising her hand for anything in the last three years, let alone speaking out loud in a group. Very few of her teammates had ever even had a long conversation with her.

She said her name was Sue. She was fifteen. That was as far as she got when she began crying again. Eventually, she spoke.

"I feel like I always have to be the best in everything I do . . . and I feel like everything is going to fall apart at any given moment. I just can't keep it all to-gether. I'm going to fail somewhere. And then what will happen? I feel so alone . . ." Then she began to cry again.

The coaches, as well as all her teammates, were stunned. No one, least of all the coaches, had any idea she was feeling that way. She had been faking her way through, while feeling completely isolated.

Sue was an honor roll student, an accomplished musician on several instru-ments—giving individual recitals and playing with the school band—and a com-mitted competitive athlete, traveling many weekends of the year to compete in away meets.

At a certain point in our conversation, I asked her coach to talk about how he felt toward her.

"Are you aware of how much I care about you?" he asked.

She shook her head no.

In a gentle voice, he apologized for not making her aware of his care and in-terest in her. He told her how much he cared for all his athletes, and how he learned long ago that the physical part of swimming—training and competing—was only one aspect of being a coach, and not the most important aspect. Then he acknowledged that he had let her down by never making her aware of how important she was to him as a person. He had failed her, he said. He apologized again. Then after a moment's hesitation, he said to her, "I love the way you play the piano . . ." It was the key to her heart.

"You know I play the piano?" she asked incredulously.

"Oh, yes," he said. "I have seen you play many times. You play so beautifully . . ." And then his eyes filled with tears.

Sue had been focusing all her energy on achievement. She did not even give herself time for relationships, on the team or off it. Nor did she value herself for anything other than her last achievement. And until that day, she believed every-one else valued her only for her achievements too. It had never occurred to her that her coach would be so moved, not by how well she played the piano, but by how the sound of her music made him feel.

Sue was clearly physically accomplished and intellectually adept in several areas. She was also emotionally suppressed, cut off from others, and felt very alone. She was way out of balance in her development as a person, causing her to feel mounting and finally overwhelming pressure at having to maintain a life defined by her achievements. She believed she was her achievements.

That day was a turning point for Sue. Many of her teammates, though few knew her as a close friend, followed their coach's lead. They raised their hands, one after the other, and spoke to her about all the things they had noticed and admired in her from a distance: her smile, her courage, her support of others during training, her lack of complaining, and her willingness to always try her hardest, whether she succeeded or not. She was so moved by their comments that she began to cry all over again.

The example of Sue is all too common in youth athletics. Certainly it is healthy to want to achieve, but how did she become so out of balance? Why did she have to break down before someone noticed? How significant a part did her parents play in determining her value system? And how can this be prevented from happening to other young athletes?

Paying close attention to all aspects of the development of the Whole Self, as opposed to focusing on just certain aspects of it, like physical achievement and intellectual prowess, is certainly one way to keep the direction of a young athlete's growth in balance.

Developing the Whole Self so it is in balance is important to young people in another significant way. The enhanced harmony it can bring to young athletes allows for a broader sense of achievement in the different aspects of a particular sport that are natural and appropriate to them as individuals. Not every athlete is going to win all the competitions, nor should they have to in order to be considered successful. What is important is how their overall athletic experience contributes to who they are becoming as people.

Young athletes are in the process of discovering who they are, as well as what they are capable of doing—that is a major part of what growing up is all about. Competitive sports can serve as a valuable avenue for this process of self-discovery—as long as it allows for and supports the nurturing and development of the Whole Self.

The Seven Components of the Whole Self

There are seven essential components to the Whole Self. They represent a balance of essential, ever-expanding, and very real parts of young people. These components are integral to how they live and experience their everyday lives, both in and out of competitive sports:

1. Physical strengths
2. Inner strengths
3. Talents
4. Intellect
5. Emotions
6. Spirit and wonder
7. Spirituality

Each component is unique, having its own special value, yet all work in harmony. The compromising of any one component can upset the synergy and balance of the entire Whole Self. What follows is a description of each component and how it functions in young athletes.

Physical Strengths

Physical strengths comprise the most tangible and obvious part of the Whole Self. This component contains everything connected to the physical doing of the sport—actions, skills, techniques, strength, size, speed, and weight. The ability to develop and use physical attributes with grace and elegance, and in coordination is what all athletes strive to achieve.

Inner Strengths

All young athletes must discover their own unique blend of inner strengths, which are derived from the innate human qualities given to all of us. These include courage, will, perseverance, and determination. There are also such traits as imagination, creativity, curiosity, humor, empathy, love, forgiveness, compassion, passion, patience, leadership, and trust. Added to this is the ability to desire, to dream, and to hope. And beyond that, there is intuition and the ability to perceive and conceive.

This process of discovery is an essential element of a young athlete's growth and maturity into adulthood. No two athletes will ever have the same blend of strengths, just as no two people will ever have the same fingerprints. For example, where one athlete may have tremendous will and determination, another might have an equally strong mix of will and patience. If both athletes pursue the same goal, each may be tenacious in his approach, but they will handle the ups and downs of pursuing that goal differently.

Perhaps the greatest beauty of one's inner strengths is that this component is where so much of a young athlete's real potential lies, for there is no limit to the power of the will, the scope of the imagination, or the magnitude of a dream.

Talents

Talents are the special and very personal attributes that each young athlete has. Each person is born with unique and quite distinct talents. For example, many young people may be able to lead, but only some will have a talent for leadership. This talent gives those who possess it something noticeably extra—such as powerful charisma. They will have an affinity, a natural sense, a gift, to lead.

Many young athletes have certain physical and emotional talents that stand out. The list is long, but here are a few examples.

- ❏ They succeed at everything they try.
- ❏ They bounce back from defeat with remarkable strength and confidence.
- ❏ They can make others feel safe.
- ❏ They inspire with their determination and perseverance. Often certain inner strengths are also talents.
- ❏ They exude passion.
- ❏ They have a knack for humor.

The development of a young athlete's talent is obviously an important key to his or her success. Yet, sometimes talents do not surface at young ages. They often show up more in the teen years rather than in preadolescence. And many people do not discover their talents until much later in life.

Intellect

The component of intellect enables young athletes to develop the ability to think and reason. Conceptualizing, figuring things out, memorizing, learning, reading, and developing the ability to speak and write are born in their intellect. Development of the intellect allows for understanding of what they see and hear in the world. Intellect is vital to their ability to organize their lives, to do their homework, and to solve various everyday problems.

Athletes use their intellect to grasp and learn technique, to set goals, and to plan out a strategy for achieving those goals. They can reflect upon and analyze feedback from a coach, communicate with teammates, and learn to understand their unique strengths and talents.

The intellect can be a trap, though. Far too often, the intellect becomes the only component of the Whole Self that a young person uses to comprehend themselves and life. The other components, because they are not always explicable or understood, often end up being ignored. If ignored long enough, components such as the emotions, and spirit and wonder, can end up being completely repressed. If they are repressed long enough, they will create a debilitating, negative effect upon the individual. In the next section on emotions, this negative effect is discussed at greater length.

Emotions

Emotions are powerful forms of live, potent energy, and they have the greatest impact upon the harmony of the Whole Self. Pent-up emotions such as anger or fear can prevent us from being able to think, feel, and even function in a normal, healthy way. At the same time, when we freely express such emotions as joy and happiness, we can lift our spirits and feed our hearts, making life seem sweeter and richer than words could ever begin to express. All emotions, whether comfortable or not, have great value.

Whereas the intellect gives meaning and understanding to life, emotions give our lives depth, feeling, substance, and a sense of being alive.

Young athletes have difficulty dealing with the emotional component of their Whole Selves, for they are rarely taught how to effectively respond to their feelings. To compound matters, they are frightened of intense emotions. Because they are too young to have developed any depth to their emotional self, intense feelings cause them to feel fearful, out of control, and confused. Suppression, avoidance, and denial become their ways of coping with uncomfortable and painful feelings. The problem is that coping in this manner, though it seems to work in the short run, eventually does far more damage than good.

It works like this. A numbed out—suppressed—emotion still has a constricting effect upon us, whether we are consciously feeling it or not. An emotion works like live energy that becomes trapped in our consciousness until it is released (experienced or felt). While it is trapped it creates a certain drain upon our entire being. The amount of drain is in direct proportion to how much emotion is being suppressed.

Young people are particularly vulnerable to this draining effect, and can only cope with so much of it. Too much drain can easily diminish their ability to function—in athletics and everywhere else in their lives.

Of all the emotions, love is the most essential to children and teens—and to the Whole Self. When children feel loved, they have an increased capacity to function more smoothly in all components of their daily lives. Any threat to, or actual loss of, that love can cause emotional turbulence.

Emotions have enormous impact upon young athletes' lives. The greatest problems they face are nearly always emotional ones.

Spirit and Wonder

Spirit and wonder are combined because they act in synergy with one another. There is no way to truly capture in words what spirit and wonder are. They exist beyond words, in feelings and senses, through joy and inspiration. They are about one's essence, and whenever anyone says, "That athlete has real heart," you know that spirit and wonder are being described.

Spirit is that part of young athletes that gives rise to their passion and enthusiasm. Passion is so essential in athletics. It helps one reach for more. Enthusiasm, on the other hand, feeds and nurtures a young athlete's energy.

Spirit might be described as the source of the inner fire that burns so brightly in many young athletes. You can see their spirit in their eyes and feel it in their excitement. It is an energy force that is undeniable, carrying with it a sense of confidence.

Wonder, very closely aligned with spirit, produces a sense of innocence and curiosity, which feeds and nurtures a young athlete's creativity. Here is where those beautiful words, "I want to try," originate. Here is also where that sense of life is born in young athletes. And that life is so valuable for it brings forth determination, which is essential in competitive athletics. All together, these aspects of wonder—innocence, curiosity, creativity, life, and determination—give young athletes their drive.

Spirit and wonder are the lifeline to personal achievement and to the fulfillment of dreams. And when allowed to soar, a single athlete's spirit and wonder can light a fire under an entire team—indeed, an entire country—as well as move to tears every competitor and every observer witnessing the event.

Spirituality

Spirituality is a distinct component of the Whole Self. It is not the Spirit, but more the source of it.

Everyone is spiritual, but we experience it, and even talk about it, in many different ways. That is because it is a personal and private experience. I do not speak of spirituality in terms of religion. It certainly can be spoken about in those terms, but I refer to it in a more personal and private way, one that has nothing to do with an organization.

Spirituality is ultimately based upon our beliefs. There are many who make another's personal beliefs "right" or "wrong." I prefer not to look at it that way. For me it is the knowledge and the feeling that I am loved and cared for by a higher being—and I always will be. That higher being is referred to by many names, God, Allah, Buddha, Goddess, Our Creator, and so forth.

In my experience, one label is no better than another. They all work. There are those who do not necessarily believe in a higher being; but they do believe that everything is connected on some level, and that they are in some way a part of that connection. This awareness gives them a source of strength. However different or alike our beliefs are, believing in a spiritual world can give us an ever-growing sense of peace and love in our lives. It is an invaluable and integral part of the development of the Whole Self, for it can give young people a sense of strength and connection to something greater than themselves. It can also offer hope, inspiration, forgiveness, a sense of worth and value, and—in a very real way—a sense of belonging that young people so desperately need. Young people can benefit greatly from developing their spiritual side.

These seven components of the Whole Self—physical strengths, inner strengths, talents, intellect, emotions, spirit and wonder, and spirituality—if nurtured and developed, give young people an opportunity to discover the beauty, the magnificence, and the very essence of who they are as human beings. Participating in competitive athletics can be a much richer and more exciting adventure when all components of the Whole Self are involved.

It might be helpful to point out that there are many highly accomplished and successful athletes—from the professional level on down—who have not focused on developing their Whole Selves. I have worked with a number of them.

They were, and many still are, able to compete at inspiring and outstanding levels, many becoming the best in their sport. On the other hand, however great athletes become, can they achieve what they are truly capable of if their Whole Selves are out of balance? In other words, how much more could they achieve, how much more harmony, synergy, and focus would they have available to them, if they had their Whole Selves to draw from? How much more natural talent could be brought to the surface? And even more important than athletic potential, how much more balanced and fulfilling would their day-to-day lives be if all components of their Whole Selves were valued and being developed?

Yes, it is possible for athletes to achieve great performances without developing their Whole Selves, but how much of who they are will be lost along the way?

The majority of this book is, in one way or another, about supporting and nurturing the Whole Self—particularly its emotional component. It is not always stated directly, as in, "This is how you support your child's Whole Self." Yet everything—whether it be about the importance of your own emotional awareness or how you listen to your children—touches directly or indirectly upon how you and others affect the development and harmony of your child's Whole Self.

The continuing development of the Whole Self is ultimately a lifelong pursuit. The more securely an early foundation is built, the easier it will be for your children to continue their own growth and development.

The Challenge of Developing the Whole Self

Hopefully, the purpose of any athletic program for young people will be to develop all components of who they are—not just their intellect or their physical strengths. Yet, as already mentioned, this is not generally the approach taken by competitive sports programs, whether in private clubs or schools. Their focus is principally on the intellect and the physical strengths, which leaves a rather large gap in a young person's overall development.

Perhaps what is most glaring in the vast majority of these programs is the lack of any sort of emotional education. Ironically, of all the components of the Whole Self, emotions are the most difficult for young people to address, and the most critical to their overall harmony. Not surprisingly, emotions are also the most difficult for teachers, coaches, and parents, to address—which might explain why they are rarely a part of educational and competitive programs.

The Need for Emotional Education

Emotional education is essential to the development of a young person's Whole Self. Suppressed and pent-up emotions can so easily debilitate—for some, even paralyze—all aspects of their abilities, athletic and otherwise. Emotional education—the process of becoming emotionally aware—is so critical that it is the major focus of this book.

The bottom line is this: You have the most influence over your children's emotional education. The more emotionally aware you are, the more you will be able to contribute to the emotional development of your child's Whole

Self. On the surface, being aware of your feelings—and knowing how to deal with them—might seem like a simple thing to do. Yet, how comfortable are most of us with intense feelings, such as pain, anger, fear, and hurt? And how many of us really know what our emotional impact upon others is? Do we talk about these things, openly and honestly, and then act upon what we discover? How often do we deny our feelings because it's easier than dealing with them?

Becoming emotionally aware is not a simple achievement. It is a complex and challenging process that takes courage, commitment, and an openness on your part to change, as well as the willingness to continually learn about and explore your feelings.

The following chapters are about helping you succeed with this challenge, so that you can be truly effective in your children's emotional education, and thus in the development of their Whole Selves.

CHAPTER 3

Imagination: A Young Person's Greatest Gift

At this very moment millions of young people all over the world are imagining who they want to be, what they want to achieve, and how they want to live. Some are lying under their covers in a warm bed, just about ready to fall asleep. Others are daydreaming while sitting in classrooms, walking on country roads, or staring up at the stars. They are expanding their world, their future, and their emerging selves by using their imagination.

Some of these young people, your children, are young athletes. They are imagining themselves jumping, shooting, throwing, swimming, running, hitting, sliding, skating, diving, flipping, and doing whatever else they do in their sport. They are stars—winning, surpassing, achieving, breaking records, laughing, and bursting with unbridled joy as they see themselves being victorious. Through their imagination they are seeding futures, building mental and emotional pathways toward these futures. They are alive, full of purpose, dreaming themselves anew.

How valuable is their imagination? Without it, who would your children become—who *could* they become?

Though we all use it, imagination itself is impossible to accurately describe or measure. It exists outside of time and human understanding. It is like trying to describe the taste of something. No matter how many times you try to describe it, no words can ever capture the actual taste itself. Yet, as with so many things of value to us—love, spirituality, joy, peace, friendship, safety, security—imagination is a very real personal experience that is unique to each of us.

Imagination is essential to just about everything we do. Look at all the things we could not do if we lost our imagination. We could no longer dream, visualize, or relate to a future of any kind. We could not feel empathy towards others, because we could not imagine what it would be like to be in their shoes. We could not change, because we could not imagine being different. Hope could not exist. Without imagination, what would there be to hope for?

The richness in the way we create our music, our art, our gardens, our homes, our cities—everything—would be diminished or lost. Life would be, well, can you even imagine it?

Yet, even with the tremendous value, richness, and future imagination offers us, by the time most young people graduate from high school, how much time have they spent learning to sharpen and expand their imagination?

School Systems Lack Imagination and Creativity

Imagination and creativity are vital to young people. They need to daydream, night dream, and pretend. They need to allow fantasy to fill and expand their minds. They need to learn how to sense the indescribable and the undefinable. All of these things are fundamental to self-discovery. Yet, our education system puts most of its emphasis on the thinking and intellectual process. Little focus is on the creative and imaginative process.

The basic courses offered in our schools are usually intellectual in nature, with the exception of physical education, music, drama, and art. These last three—which are usually electives—do contribute to developing creativity and imagination, but they have been the first courses to be discontinued all across the nation whenever there are budget cuts.

What about private schools? Even there, how many courses that help develop creativity and imagination are offered—and are required courses?

Without a chance to develop and sharpen their sense of creativity and imagination, our young people will face a future without the scope, depth, insight, and feeling that could be there if they had a more balanced foundation of education. Intellectual prowess alone can never provide these things.

That is where competitive athletics can offer an opportunity.

Competitive Sports: Sharpening Creativity and Imagination

Fortunately, competitive sports can offer young people a chance to go outside of logic, to discover, create, dream, and fantasize. Sports are not structured like academics. The athletic experience is very much a personal one that is indescribable and full of emotion—from the heights of joy to the depths of pain. It is an opportunity for self-discovery that can utilize a great deal of imagination. It calls upon learning from within, done by feel and senses. It is in many ways pure personal creativity, for even though athletes can be taught, they must "create" the movements themselves.

Because it is such a personal and internal experience, competitive sports gives athletes a tremendous opportunity to sharpen their creativity and imagination.

Visualization Can Be a Young Athlete's Greatest Tool

One of the most common, yet most powerful, tools that brings so much of the creative and imaginative process into play is something all athletes of all ages do—visualization.

Young athletes are used to focusing on their performance, mentally, emotionally, and physically. Their desire to improve, to learn, and to win fuels their imagination. They are constantly "practicing" their sports outside the physical arena using visualization. They see themselves winning or achieving what they want or trying out a new movement, shot, stroke, swing, etc. They visualize in their daydreams, their night dreams, during their school classes, on the way to competitions, everywhere and anywhere. They are in the world of their imagination becoming the athletes they aspire to be.

When athletes train and compete they use visualization as a tool to help them improve, change momentum, win, or to accomplish anything else they are trying to achieve. Visualizing comes naturally to them, like breathing.

There is great power in visualization. By visualizing themselves doing physical movements, athletes are in effect training their muscles and their brains—as if they are physically practicing. The more one visualizes specific physical movements, the more the neuronal pathways in the brain that control the patterning of those muscles are developed and reinforced.

Visualization is so real that athletes commonly feel the movements they are seeing, their muscles often contracting and twitching in accordance with what they are visualizing.

Positive Thinking vs. Visualization

Many people confuse visualization with positive thinking. They are significantly different from each other, though they can cross over into each other's territory.

Athletes have heard about "positive thinking" for years. The term is so common it has become a cliche. Yet, there is a general misunderstanding about what it really is.

Positive thinking, in short, is thinking positively. It is an intellectual exercise, not about feeling or imagining. It is about holding positive thoughts, with the idea in mind that those thoughts will create a positive future.

Many believe, and here is where the misunderstanding lies, that positive thinking means if you think no "negative" thoughts, you will automatically have only "positive" thoughts. The problem with this concept of positive thinking is simple. Is it possible to keep all negative thoughts out of your mind? That includes anxiety, fear, and doubt. Ever try it? That is akin to my telling you, "Do not think about pink elephants." What just went through your mind?

Consider this example. Remember that time you really wanted your child to win that contest or competition? How much anxiety did you have, especially when it got closer to the event? You might even have felt supremely confident—yet still felt anxiety, for you know nothing is guaranteed.

Here is why that happens. When you are studiously trying to avoid thinking about something, by your very effort to avoid that something you are in effect keeping it in your thoughts. And the harder you try not thinking about something, the more you usually end up thinking about it. That is the problem—and the flaw—with this concept of positive thinking.

Positive thinking in the framework of never having negative thoughts simply does not work. You do have doubts, fears, and insecurities—especially when something is very important to you—and you cannot keep them from entering your mind. This is particularly true of young people, who can be very frightened and emotionally ungrounded. If you were to look at positive thinking in a different way, in terms of trying your best to look for what could go right while acknowledging your fears and doubts and attempting to reduce them, then "positive thinking" has merit.

Visualization, so different from positive thinking, brings your imagination, your emotions, and many of your other senses into play, as opposed to just your intellect. As with positive thinking, there is an ineffective and an effective way to visualize.

Just visualizing something—without feeling—is not a very effective process. The key to successful visualizations, in which you create neural pathways in your brain to the future you want, is to feel your emotions intensely while you are visualizing. In other words, when you visualize yourself doing something you are excited about or that you want to achieve in the future, feel excited! Feel joyful, happy, grateful, exuberant! Feel every emotion with as much intensity as you can.

Your subconscious responds to images and feelings more strongly than just to thoughts, because there is much more electromagnetic energy around them. The more energy—intense feelings—you bring into your visualization, the more you imprint your subconscious and brain with them.

Try this exercise as a way to compare the difference between positive thinking and visualization. Close your eyes and think, "I am winning, I am winning, I am winning" for one minute. How much energy did it take to do that?

Now close your eyes and see—visualize—yourself or your child winning for one minute. Do not think anything—just feel—with intensity, all the emotions of joy, excitement, happiness, and exuberance that you would feel if you or your child really did win.

Look at the difference between the two exercises. You will notice that when you visualize while feeling intensely, it takes a lot more energy and has a much more powerful impact upon you than when you just "think positively."

The key here, once again, is that visualizing with intense feeling creates a source of energy that imprints the subconscious and creates a bridge to a future event. You are creating the feeling of already having done that event.

Though thinking positively, when done appropriately, does have merit, it cannot create the intense energy that your imagination and feelings can. It alone cannot create a strong bridge to a future event.

Creating a "Future Self"

How many times have you heard a champion say they have been "visualizing this moment for years"? Athletes use their imagination not only to pattern their muscles and brains, but also to create their "Future Selves"—the ones who have already achieved that specific goal or goals. That Future Self may be days or several years out into the future. It is this Future Self, held vividly in the imagination and the emotions, who gives the present-day athlete the inspiration, courage, and will to continue toward that future.

Some might think that Future Selves are just made up, things of our imagination—yes, exactly!—our imagination. Remember, the brain does not know the difference between imagined and physical acts. By repeatedly visualizing a particular future, a young person is creating a real and viable pathway into that future. All young athletes have Future Selves out there, not in the sense of being predestined, but as possibilities. It is up to them to guide themselves toward the futures of their choice. Through visualization and emotional intensity, they are doing just that.

I talk to many young athletes, as well as college and professional athletes, about their Future Selves. We work on how to visualize and create the atmosphere that will best help them feel and sense that future as alive and real as possible. They all respond very positively, particularly to the feelings it gives them. They feel more confident and prepared for who they want to become.

The idea of a Future Self is a powerful concept to introduce to young people. It is not a guarantee that everything will automatically work out, but it can be a vital component of every athlete's overall training. The Future Self can become a very real part of a young athlete's imagination, giving hope and building confidence.

A Guided Visualization/Meditation
For Young Athletes

Visualization is so important to the development of young people's imagination that I have created a special visualization/meditation audio tape. It will help them sharpen their imagination, create their Future Selves, and learn to relax their bodies, where so much natural healing can then take place.

First, it is important to look at what meditation is, for it is different from visualization. Meditation, in simple terms, is a relaxed state of mind and body that alters our consciousness. Every single person alive meditates every day, several times, though most of the time it is not done consciously.

Daydreaming, night dreaming, or wandering off mentally while walking down the street are all forms of meditation. Every time you relax, ride in a car on a long trip in silence, get totally absorbed in your gardening or anything else, or disappear deeply into your thoughts, you are altering your state of consciousness. You are meditating.

Young people meditate all the time. They daydream everywhere they are, wandering off mentally in classes, during lunch, dinner, while doing homework, or while waiting for a bus or ride. And even when young athletes warm up for training or competition, they often go into an altered state of consciousness, becoming very internally focused as they mentally and emotionally prepare themselves.

Visualization—imagining/seeing/picturing/sensing/feeling—on the other hand, differs from meditation in that it is an activity that is done *while* meditating. Visualizing can be done with eyes open or closed. You see athletes visualize with their eyes open before events all the time. They are seemingly oblivious to everything around them as they focus on what they are seeing in their minds.

It is easier to hold a continual focus for a longer time, though, if your eyes are closed. There are fewer distractions, which allows for complete focus and uninterrupted emotional intensity. This intensity becomes like a beam of light, boring into the subconscious and the brain, imprinting them with far greater effect.

All young athletes visualize and meditate, but not all know how to do it in the most effective way. They are for the most part doing what comes naturally to them, but there are very effective ways to work with the subconscious that they may not be aware of. The keys to successful visualization/meditations are relaxation, focus, graphic imagination, feeling with intensity, and repetition. The audio tape, "The Emerald Lagoon," was created to help young athletes do all these things, and a little more.

36

"The Emerald Lagoon"

"The Emerald Lagoon" is an imaginative, graphically descriptive, and fun visualization/meditation. The visualization includes a sandy beach, a warm sun, a moss-covered rock pathway, a shallow cave behind a waterfall, and a beautiful emerald-green lagoon. It is easy to follow and very relaxing. At a certain place, there is an opportunity to visualize anything an athlete wants to create. Directions are included, though all that is needed is to listen.

All the natural elements, water, fire (seen as the sun), air, and earth, are purposely included in the visualization because they offer such an effective way of speaking to deeper parts of us, pulling us even more into our imagination.

This tape is a valuable tool to help young athletes sharpen their creative and imaginative skills, and to help them create the Future Self of their dreams. It is geared specifically to young athletes because they respond to and enjoy visualization. It also helps you add imaginative balance to their education.

"The Emerald Lagoon" can also be used for any other dreams they want to pursue. It is about creativity and imagination—of any sort. And if they just want to relax, they can do that with it too.

It is interesting to note that many parents have used the tape and have enjoyed it as much as their kids.

If you would like to have a tape sent to you for your child, please refer to page 171 of the book for directions.

Parents and Parenting

CHAPTER 4

The Far-Reaching Effects of a Parent's Love

There came a point in my life when I realized that most of the decisions I had made about my sense of value and self-worth were based upon my relationship with my parents. That seems rather obvious now in looking back, but the scope of their influence was not at all obvious then. How they treated me, how they spoke to me, and how often they positively or negatively acknowledged me, all had a tremendous effect upon me. Their behavior toward me was central in shaping how I felt about myself. Those feelings ended up having enormous impact upon the rest of my life.

Some of my feelings about myself were positive, but most were about my feeling "not good enough" in one way or another. So much of my motivation was to gain my parent's acknowledgment and approval and to be "good enough" in their eyes. I wanted my parents to be proud of me. If I failed to gain approval, I tried harder. I also rebelled and disagreed, acted arrogant, and did all the normal things kids do, but underneath it all, the thing I wanted most was for my mother and father to love me and to care about what I did.

Everywhere I go, the young people I speak with, to varying degrees, feel just as I did. Some kids are more secure with their parents than others, but all kids, secure or not, look to their parents for approval and acceptance. And all of them are tremendously hurt if their parents judge, ignore, or demean them in any way. Such things as self-worth, self-esteem, and personal value can be strongly bolstered, or they can take a real beating, depending upon the attitude and actions of a father or mother.

The First Source of Love

It is certainly understandable that we are so strongly affected by our parents. As small children we are all totally dependent on them for our survival and security. Every thought and feeling we have is intertwined with our parents' thoughts and feelings. We are simply too young to be independent of them. As we become teenagers, we begin the process of separating from our parents. We have to; we need to discover our own identities. But at the same time, it is impossible to completely dissociate our thoughts, feelings, and beliefs from those of our parents. Years of living with them, loving them, needing them, rebelling against them, and being exposed to all the other things that go on in parent-child relationships have a dominating influence upon us.

It is our parents' influence that has the most determining impact upon our concepts of self-love, self-worth, and self-esteem. We are vulnerable to all their actions and to everything they say to us. And we are always interpreting, correctly or incorrectly, how they feel and what they are thinking about us, which affects how we feel about ourselves.

Here is an example of one father's behavior toward his son:

After a Parent's Seminar, a rather anxious mother approached me and asked if I would speak to her husband. He did not know she was going to bring me back to talk to him. As we approached him, I could see his obvious surprise. Clearly, he did not consider asking me anything. This was her idea.

She began by telling me how afraid her son, Bob, who was eleven, had become over the last three years. He seemed to have lost all of his former confidence. He was a good athlete, she said, but it seemed he was reluctant to give it a hundred percent in competitions.

The father began saying how disappointed he was in his son. He did not understand why his son seemed to have lost his motivation—he was wasting his talent.

As we talked about their son and how he approached his practices and competitions, the father was intense and outspoken, harsh in his disappointment over Bob's failures. The mother seemed to be always trying to calm him down, being the voice of reason and understanding. After fifteen minutes or so into our conversation, the mother seemed to have had enough of her husband's tone and attitude toward their son. She suddenly blurted out that she knew exactly where her son's loss of confidence had begun. It was when he was in the third grade, she said, right around the time when be began exhibiting signs of losing his confidence.

She then related what had happened. The son was always a good student, excelling in every subject except English. He had never really been interested in English. It was just one of those subjects he found boring, the mother said. One day after taking a test he went to class and the teacher read the scores out loud, like she always did. Bob was shocked that he had scored so low. The teacher, as was her habit, had everyone with a poor grade sit in the back of the room. They would stay there until they improved their grades. That way everyone knew who did what. The teacher may have believed this was a good way to motivate someone, but she did not seem to care if they were humiliated in the process.

Indeed, Bob came home from school feeling humiliated and embarrassed. He told his mom and dad what had happened and said he did not want to stay in the back of the room. His father immediately showed his disappointment over Bob's performance. He told him, "You will study every night until you improve your grades!"

For the next several weeks the father sat with his son every night, going over his English homework with him. The mother said the pressure the father put on Bob to improve his grades was intense and unrelenting. It seemed to her that her husband had become so driven to help his son get a better grade that if Bob did not do better it would be a personal defeat for his father. And she was sure, as she watched Bob's reaction every night during homework sessions, that he felt the same way.

She tried, she said, to get her husband to back off, but he would not. It had become a personal challenge. The father was going to make sure his son was not someone who sat in the back of a classroom because of a low grade. She told her husband what she was seeing in Bob: his fear, his increased anxiety as midterms drew closer. She told her husband he was pressuring Bob, but he ignored her.

Midterm exams finally came, and the test scores were read out loud. Bob's score was worse than his first one. He was devastated. His father was angry.

His father confronted him. "What is wrong?" he asked. "You have talent. You studied. Why aren't you doing better?"

As the mother recalled, the father redoubled his efforts to help his son study. "You can do this!" he told Bob. The homework sessions became more intense. And Bob's scores, if anything, became worse. He remained in the back of the class for the rest of the semester, much to his father's disappointment.

His grades in his other classes were fine, but he was never able to earn even average scores in any English class ever since then. And something else began happening.

Little by little, Bob's demeanor changed. He seemed to lose his general sense of excitement, his enthusiasm. The mother said it seemed like he began holding back his drive to achieve, to succeed. When he joined the swimming team two years ago, though excited at first, he always seemed to play it safe in his workouts and competitions, never really going all out.

The father involved himself in Bob's athletics as he had in his English homework—with intensity and high expectations. His way of supporting him was to yell at him, as if somehow he could make him try harder by the sheer force of his voice. He would again ask him what was wrong, telling him he could do better. Bob would only say, "I'm trying . . . ."

As the mother was talking, I was remembering Bob, who was in the seminar earlier that day. His eyes were mostly downcast, and he rarely raised his hand or offered anything of himself. But the one time he did speak, he said he felt like he could never be good enough for his father.

As the mother finished her story I asked the father if he also noticed Bob's change in demeanor. He did, and added, "I know I may have been too hard on him during his English homework. I know that he seemed to hold back after that."

As we spoke, it was clear the father felt very guilty and responsible for what had happened. He said the worst part was that he realized he was doing just what his father had done to him when he was a boy—pressuring his son to do more.

The three of us talked about what to do next. The father knew he had to ease up in his treatment of Bob. He also knew he needed to tell Bob that he was not at fault for his father's actions. I offered to set up a conference between parents and son, but the father said he could handle this himself, that he needed to.

He agreed to follow through. Both mother and father thanked me for listening and left.

The coach saw me speaking with the parents and knew it was about the father's treatment of Bob. He said he was very aware of the father's behavior—and its effect upon Bob. He said he had spoken to the father on a number of occasions, but nothing he could say seemed to have any effect upon the father's behavior.

Two weeks later I followed up with the coach on Bob's father. For one week the coach had noticed a real difference in the father's behavior. He was less vocal, less agitated, and less angry, but by the end of the second week he was right back to his old ways.

How do children feel when they are treated the way Bob's father treated him? What do they decide about their value and self-worth? You can pretty well guess. They feel shamed, flawed, scared of failure—and even more scared of success because then there is even more to lose. They can easily become perfectionists, feeling if they can just be "perfect," no one will see the flaw that their parents obviously see—and continually remind them of. They end up suppressing their emotions as a way to stop the pain they feel at being humiliated and rejected by their parents. And, over time, they build up a lot of rage, anger, and hurt, which eventually leaks—or bursts—out into their relationships and everyday lives.

It is vital when loving children and teens, particularly when there are extra pressures put upon them in the world of competitive sports, to become aware of what feelings you are expressing to them. Do you think it is patience and love, while it is really frustration? Or perhaps you think you can hide your anger or disappointment in them, but you are really communicating those feelings through your facial expression and tone of voice. Maybe you believe that if you do not say anything, they will somehow be unaware of what you are really feeling. Whatever the scenario, the key is trying to be as aware as possible of what emotional impact you are having on your children, and to ask yourself, is this the impact I want to have?

What you feel and express—whether you are aware of it or not—does have a direct effect upon your children. The more aware you are of your emotional impact, the more you can be responsible for it, meaning you can consciously make sure your guidance, discipline, support, and love is as positive, reassuring, and consistent as possible.

Providing for and protecting your children are primary responsibilities of all parents, but "emotionally" loving your children—being emotionally responsible for how you relate to them—is what will have the greatest and most long-lasting influence upon how they think and feel about themselves.

"Emotionally" Loving Your Children

There are a number of parents who assume they are emotionally loving their children, though they have never learned how to responsibly deal with their own emotions. Many are full of anger and rage. They punish their kids for the smallest mistake—with words, a look, or a tone of voice. These parents have been suppressing their emotions for years to escape their own pains and emotional conflicts. And now their kids are paying the price for their parents' unwillingness to respond to their own emotional needs.

It is quite impossible to be emotionally responsible in how you relate to your children if you suppress your feelings. Suppressing feelings means refusing to recognize them. You cannot be emotionally suppressed and emotionally responsible at the same time.

There are also those parents who are much more aware of what they are feeling. And they try to *stay* aware when they relate to their kids. They know how much their own feelings influence their children.

Whether you are a parent who is already emotionally loving your children, or you are one who knows you need to begin learning how to do it, the goal is the same: to love in such a way that makes your children feel valuable, worthy, and lovable, just as they are.

Another way of saying this is to love your children in a way that makes them feel emotionally secure—and that can be done only with emotional responsibility.

Learning how to become more emotionally aware—which will give you the ability to be more emotionally responsible—is discussed in some detail in Section Three, beginning with Chapter Eight, "The Complexity of Emotions."

CHAPTER 5

Providing Emotional Security

Because you, as a parent, have the greatest emotional influence upon your children, you become their primary source of emotional learning. You are also the one who has the greatest responsibility in providing their emotional security.

What does "providing emotional security" mean? It means you provide to your child, with conscious awareness and intent, a continual sense of love, understanding, patience, encouragement, acceptance, and forgiveness. It also means you do your best to protect your children from passing your emotional baggage down to them.

It is not emotionally secure, for example, when a parent ridicules, judges, humiliates, shames, or abuses a child when that child makes a mistake or fails to meet the expectations of the parent.

This might seem rather obvious. Yet, how many people take the time to learn how to effectively deal with their own emotions—to provide emotional security for themselves? How many of us are even curious as to why we feel and act the way we do, or why we react so strongly in certain situations? How much of the time are we really aware of our emotional impact upon another, particularly a child? How many of us have recognized our emotional patterns and make a concerted effort to change the ones that are self-destructive or negative and hurtful toward others?

Though you are not responsible for your children's adult lives, you do have enormous influence upon their most difficult, painful, and impressionable years. Providing emotional security for them in their childhood and adolescence can make a tremendous difference in their ability to provide emotional security for themselves in their adult lives.

It would seem natural that providing emotional security for children would be a high priority for any parent. For the vast majority it is, but that does not necessarily mean it is an easy thing to learn how to do—or that the majority of parents are successfully doing it.

We Were Never Taught How to Feel

Whenever I ask a roomful of parents how many of them, on a daily or even on a weekly or monthly basis, take the time to sit down and deal with whatever fears, angers, hurts, and pain they might be feeling, rarely more than a few hands are raised. Most laugh out loud at the apparent absurdity of the question. It is as if taking the time to respond to their emotions, to nurture themselves, to clear up any pent-up feelings, is a foreign concept.

In one seminar a woman actually reacted to the question by suddenly bursting out in a loud, angry voice, "I haven't got time for feelings—I'm raising two kids!" Everyone in the room, including myself, went into a stunned silence. Even she seemed to have shocked herself with her outburst.

Delicately, I asked her who was getting all the rage that she did not have the time to deal with—the rage everyone in the room just felt from her.

She was silent for a long, reflective moment. Then she said, "My kids."

"Are they?" I asked.

"Yes . . . they are . . ." she finally answered in a barely audible voice.

"Who else might be getting it besides them?" I then asked.

"Well, when I think about it, I guess everyone who is close to me is getting it," she said. Then she added, somewhat stunned by her own growing awareness, "I never knew I felt so much rage."

She was very open and vulnerable and talked about how she had become lost in her and her children's myriad of day-to-day chores and activities, until she felt like she had no time for herself. While talking about it, she realized that this was the source of her rage. She had never seen it until that moment—though she now knew that she had been feeling it for quite some time.

Other parents in the room began raising their hands. They spoke of how her conversation and openness had helped them to become more aware of what they were feeling. Then we all talked about how easy it was to become numb to what we were feeling when we spent all our time "doing" our lives. Focusing on feelings somehow did not seem important enough to take the time to do.

It was a fascinating and eye-opening (as well as heart-opening) discussion for everyone, led, ironically, by a woman who up until then had no conscious awareness of how emotionally pent-up she had become. Everyone left the room more sober and much more aware of their feelings.

The example of this mother, and the other parents' reaction to her, is not an uncommon incident. In every state and country I have visited, I have encountered numerous parents who ended up discovering, often being surprised by, pent-up emotions they were not consciously aware of. Many began crying when they discovered their hurt or sadness. Others expressed long-suppressed fear over their ability to be good parents. Some talked about their guilt over how they had treated their children during past angry moments. Others spoke about their fears of an impending—or a past—divorce and what it was going to do to their children's future. Most of them, many for the first time, took an honest look at how much their own emotions had been, and still were, affecting their children.

Why do so few parents—why do so few adults, parents or not, for that matter—consciously deal with their feelings? It is not a difficult question to answer. We were raised in the same society and taught in the same kind of schools that exist today, where thinking and intellect were highly valued—and feelings and emotions were controlled and hidden.

Girls were allowed to express their feelings by crying. No matter what girls felt, whether it be anger, disappointment, hurt or rage, they were expected to squeeze all their feelings into crying. Boys were judged to be weak if they showed any emotion other than anger. Tears were absolutely unacceptable. How many of us can still remember hearing the words, "big boys don't cry"? How many fathers can still hear those words in the back of their minds, spoken long ago by their fathers?

In addition, all other major aspects of the society we were raised in—medical, political, law, trade, finance, and business—also focused only on the intellect, completely avoiding any real expression of emotion. Logic, intelligence, problem solving, that's what was important. Emotions were those areas of discomfort we were supposed to intellectualize, rationalize, and distance ourselves from.

We were taught how to emotionally fit into society—to look and act the right way. The rule was to always stay in control—deny, suppress, and avoid uncomfortable feelings. Always give the appearance that everything was okay. That was the appropriate and expected way to act.

Yet somehow, in the midst of all this, we were also supposed to magically figure out how to cope with our feelings. How was that possible when at the same time we were being taught to avoid them?

The Cost of Being Emotionally Uneducated

Learning about our emotions does not just happen, any more than intellectual awareness just happens. Yet, the education system and society that most of us were raised in denied and devalued the emotional side of us. There was no emotional education available, even at the most elementary level. The cost of that lack of education has been dramatic. A vast percentage of our current adult population is emotionally uneducated and, thus, ill-equipped to effectively deal with many everyday conflicts in their families and business relationships.

How many of us have even a rudimentary awareness of how to deal effectively with common emotions such as anger, hurt, fear, love, frustration, or anxiety? And of those of us who do know how to deal with our emotions, how many of us do it on a regular basis—every day?

We learned as children and teens how to suppress and avoid painful and uncomfortable feelings. And because we were young, feelings were frightening and beyond our depth of understanding. We developed emotional patterns of behavior—self-pity, suppression, avoidance, numbing out to our feelings, staying busy so we would not feel—that helped us survive, so we could somehow get through the turmoil and confusion in our young lives. Our society and educational system encouraged those patterns by never offering any real alternatives. These emotional patterns (habits of control, suppression, and avoidance) may have helped us get through the difficult spots in our youth, but they had a significant down side. They became a way of life. And unless we have consciously changed them, we are still suppressing and avoiding certain uncomfortable and painful feelings. The danger here is that we can suppress feelings until they disappear from our awareness completely. Why is that so dangerous? Though we may not be aware of our suppressed feelings, they still exist—and are influencing our actions and thought process without our knowing it.

Where do all of our suppressed feelings go? They do not just disappear into thin air, and the old adage "out of sight, out of mind" unfortunately does not apply to emotions.

Suppressed emotions will always, in one way or another, have an impact upon the way we relate to others. Some of us end up staying on the surface with our emotions, feeling a little here and there—not letting anyone, including ourselves, get close to our real, deeper feelings. Others of us are completely cut off from our feelings—we literally do not feel much of anything anymore. We do not know we are numbing out our emotions, but it will be quite obvious to anyone around us who is emotionally aware.

Then there are those of us who use logic to explain everything—even our feelings, which are not based on logic. This can drive people around us crazy. And all of us can easily end up leaking—or dumping—our suppressed feelings all over the ones closest to us, in the form of flashes of anger, hostility, resentment, blame, and bitterness.

And beyond this, suppressing feelings over a period of time can create health problems. Depression, suppressed anger, intense feelings of shame, deep hurt, constant fear, all can have debilitating effects upon our autoimmune system, which is our greatest defense system against disease. We are far more vulnerable to illness when our immune system is compromised.

Several well-known doctors have written best-selling books about the impact suppressed emotions have upon our health. Dr. Bernie S. Siegel, in *Peace, Love, and Healing,* goes into great detail when mentioning the amount of research being done around the world on the link between emotional suppression and disease. Dr. Andrew Weil, in *Spontaneous Healing,* talks about how feeling our emotions intensely can activate our own natural healing system. And Dr. Dean Ornish, in *Love & Survival, 8 Pathways to Intimacy and Health,* states, "When you feel loved, nurtured, cared for, supported, and intimate, you are much more likely to be happier and healthier. You have a much lower risk of getting sick and, if you do, a much greater chance of surviving." He goes on to offer the results of several medical research projects that clearly demonstrate how the relationship with our parents can directly affect our health.

As a society, as families, and as individuals, we are for the most part uncomfortable when it comes to dealing with our emotions. We do not question or even think about our denials and our long-established emotional patterns, not because we are irresponsible or immature, but because that is what we have been taught. That is what we see so many others doing, and that is what we have been willing to accept.

But we do not have to continue in this direction. We do have a choice. With desire and will we can change our emotional patterns, no matter how long they have been with us.

The Need to Change Our Emotional Patterns

Our original emotional patterns, which were based upon child and adolescent experiences, served an invaluable purpose. They helped to get us through the early part of our lives. But our early patterns were not meant to serve as the foundation for the rest of our lives. As we grew older we needed to develop new, more appropriate patterns, ones that would allow us to move into adulthood.

The problem is that during our adolescence, early and later, we rarely thought about what we decided, and we rarely questioned why we acted the way we did. We were too busy getting through life, trying to grow up. We ended up getting stuck with certain patterns of behavior that still very much exist in our lives today.

Once while I was visiting a college team, the coach approached me about a unique problem he was facing. On his team was a 19-year-old woman, Maegan, who seemed quite reluctant to become close with her teammates. Her coach was concerned and perplexed. Maegan took no part in any of the team's social activities and made no attempt to get to know anyone on the team. She was polite, a nice person, and very committed to her sport. Her teammates wanted to accept her, but they had a difficult time doing so because she would not give them a chance to get to know her better.

At the coach's request, I asked Maegan if we could talk, hoping to discover clues about her behavior. Maegan was aware of her reluctance to get close to anyone. She had always been a loner, she said. Yet, she was also aware that others felt she did not care about them, or the team. She did care, she said, but she had no way to express her feelings—without becoming closer to them. She knew she had no real friends on the team and no one really knew her, yet she had no idea what to do about it.

As we talked about her life in general and the previous teams she had competed for, it became clear that she refused to be emotionally involved with anyone on any team she joined.

There came a point in our conversation when I noticed her breathing had become fast and irregular. Just talking to her about becoming close to others, particularly girls, was causing a physical reaction in her. The longer we spoke, the more agitated she became. Suddenly she just stopped speaking. Tears filled her eyes. She looked at me as if she did not understand why she was crying. We sat in silence for a few minutes. I then asked her, with no preamble or warning, "What happened to you, Maegan?"

For whatever reason, the question, maybe because she did not expect it, seemed to jar her back into reality.

She began to cry—bucketsful. Several moments went by before she spoke.

"I had forgotten all about it until now. I was twelve when it happened," she began.

She had two very close friends, she said. The three of them were never separated from each other. They saw each other every day during school and then after school if they weren't competing in sports or studying. They talked about everything. These were her first real friendships, she added.

One day, she came home from school and called one of her friends on the phone, like she had on so many other days. For some strange reason, the friend acted like she did not know her, like she was a stranger. Maegan asked her why she was acting this way, but the friend did not change her behavior. So she called her other friend to tell her what had happened. The other friend acted just like the first one, as if she did not know her. Maegan became angry and asked what they were doing. She finally hung up out of frustration.

Each day, during school and after school, Maegan approached her friends, but they still pretended they did not know her. She became more angry and more hurt as each day passed.

She began to question herself—and her friendships. She wondered what she could have done wrong to make them want to hurt her like this. The more she questioned, the more convinced she became that something must be wrong with her. It must somehow be her fault that they decided to treat her this way. During the entire time, she never told her parents anything was wrong. She said she felt too stupid and embarrassed to tell them.

On the sixth day she hit an emotional wall. She had come to believe it was all her fault and made the decision to pull away from them, to end the friendships. She reasoned that they would not be able to continue hurting her anymore if she acted like she did not care.

Several days after that her girl friends noticed their prank was not working anymore and approached her, laughing, telling all about their little game. They said they thought it would be funny if they pretended they did not know her, just to see what she would do. They thought her reaction was so funny they decided to continue the game for several days. But now, they said, she had obviously caught on, so they wanted to resume their normal friendship again.

She looked them right in the eye and said, "What little game?" Then she turned around and walked away, leaving them standing there with their mouths open. They tried calling her for several days, apologizing, begging her to forgive them. She would not. After a week of calls they stopped trying. She never spoke to them again.

Until the day we spoke, Maegan had completely suppressed the memories of this painful incident. She had also forgotten that she had made a decision never to let anyone get close to her again—which explained why she would not allow her current teammates an opportunity to get to know her. She realized she had not had a close friendship in seven years. She had been alone, cut off and separate, for her entire adolescence.

She also realized she was indirectly punishing her 12-year-old girlfriends by holding onto her pain and never letting anyone else get close to her. She had been silently suffering for seven years.

This young woman began to change her life after our conversation and subsequent conversations with her coach. If it had not been for that caring coach, and for Maegan's courage to look at herself, she would most likely have spent the rest of her life acting out her seven-year-old pain and holding to her decision to cut herself off from all close relationships.

I cannot begin to count the number of parents I have met or know of—many of them former athletes who have had similar experiences to Maegan's—who are living out their lives through painful decisions made at young ages. Everyone around them can see it; they cannot. Many have never even thought about why they act the way they do, or how much it affects their children. Others are aware of their actions, yet refuse to change, usually blaming those around them for the state of their lives. Some of these parents have become quite hostile—acting out their hostility as they would have when they were thirteen years old—when another parent or a coach has suggested that their behavior is having a detrimental effect on their children.

Though there may be nothing obvious about your behavior and its effect on your children, how closely do you look at it? How aware are you of your impact?

Have you looked at what messages you are giving your children about love, relationships, and emotional responsibility? How much of your emotional patterning is still anchored in your past? How emotionally safe are you making it for your children? Do you really know?

Well, the truth is we all carry emotional issues with us. It is a normal part of being human. If we do not know ourselves well enough to recognize those issues, we can always learn. Clearly some people have much more to deal with than others, but all of us have issues in our lives. An essential part of our responsibility in becoming adults is to respond to our own issues, whatever they might be. It is this very process of discovery and healing that allows us to grow, understand, and learn to love ourselves, and thus develop compassion, empathy, and love for others—particularly for children and teens.

The adult world demands more responsibility than the world of our childhood and adolescence did, especially when it comes to our emotions. If we do not recognize and then change our emotional patterns, we will force everyone around us to deal with them. That includes children and teens, who are highly impressionable and cannot protect themselves from us.

CHAPTER 6

Relating
to Your
Children

This book is about relating and relationships—specifically how you relate to yourself, your spouse, your own parents, and your children. This is where the real responsibility for raising children begins.

Ultimately, you carry the greatest responsibility for the development of your children. It is not a light responsibility, but one that requires great courage and love.

It also requires an open mind, flexibility, and a willingness to change and grow, particularly when you face the added responsibility of having children who are involved in athletics.

There are many questions you face, such as: How do you view competition? What is a healthy attitude to have as a young athlete? How do you make sure that your children's experience of winning and losing is one that is as self esteem-enhancing and positive as possible? And how do you incorporate the disappointments, losses, failures, and pressures of competitive sports into the healthy development of a son or daughter? All of these questions and many more are ones that you must deal with when you take on the responsibility of raising a child who enters competitive sports.

The majority of parents I meet try to be supportive and protective of their children in every way possible. They want them to develop in a healthy, balanced manner. Yet, as loving as most parents might be, there will always be hurts, angers, misunderstandings, issues of growing up, and other such things that will impact their relationship with their children.

Are most parents aware of their emotional impact, how they are influencing their children? Generally speaking, some certainly are, but the majority are not. Many are simply too unwilling—or too afraid—to take an honest look at their behavior.

In the Parent's Seminars, parents ask questions about their behavior all the time. Many are vulnerable and want honest answers. They want to know their impact and how to change it if it is not as positive as it could be. Yet, just as many are too frightened to hear frank feedback. They would rather have an on-the-surface, quick-fix answer, one that will not make them look "bad" to others in the room.

Some Parents Are More Willing to Change

There are always individuals who do not fall into any group, but generally speaking, I meet three types of parents. The first type is very emotionally suppressed and cannot or will not change. Nor can they hear anything negative about themselves. Many of these parents become hostile when anyone—another parent, myself, a coach, their son or daughter—directly approaches them about their behavior. They tend to become righteous and defensive and sometimes very angry, saying, "Who are *you* to tell me?"

The second group is more aware of their negative patterns of behavior. They are genuinely concerned about their impact upon their kids, and they want to change whatever they can to become more supportive and loving. These parents, for the most part, are willing to learn, but they do not necessarily know where to start or how to go about it.

The third group of parents know they carry emotional patterns from their past. These parents consciously work at changing themselves, wanting to minimize whatever they might pass down to their children. Though they are very busy, particularly being parents of young athletes, they continually find ways—through seminars, books, audio tapes, groups, counseling—to learn about themselves. They look at their personal growth and the need to grow out of past emotional patterns as a necessity and a responsibility of being a parent.

The highest percentage of parents I speak with fall into the second group.

Whatever group you might identify with, or even if you do not identify with any group, you face what every parent faces—you cannot help passing on certain feelings and patterns of behavior to your children. How you love, how you fight, how you express or avoid certain feelings, how often you laugh—all the things you do influence your children. The quality of that influence—how positive or negative it is—depends upon how willing you are to grow beyond, to let go of and change, your past negative emotional patterns. The more emotionally honest, aware, and responsible you are, the greater your ability to have a conscious and positive effect on your children.

Questioning your behavior towards your children, even though you may not always feel comfortable with what you discover, is one of the essential steps of being a loving and effective parent. The willingness to then *change* your behavior because you feel it will make you a better parent is also an essential part of nurturing and loving your children. Without change you would remain exactly as you were whenever you decided life was too painful or confusing to bear emotionally, or you simply did not want to be responsible for your actions—which could have been at ten, fifteen, or twenty years of age. Think of the consequences of that.

You would not be able to feel any more deeply, care with any more insight, or understand with any deeper compassion than you did at that age. You would become a book with only one chapter.

Change is essential to all growth—your life is predicated upon it. You are born to go forward, to expand, to grow, in everything you do. If you are not willing to change, eventually you will become stiff and brittle, unable to be spontaneous, afraid of anything new and different. Ultimately, if you are unwilling to change, you will suffocate your ability to grow in any capacity.

Nearly every parent I have ever met agrees that positive change is an inherent and healthy part of life. At the same time, I have also met innumerable parents who seemingly change little in their lives. Many are unhappy, full of stress, overworked, and have difficulty communicating with their spouses and their children. They exhibit little desire to look at their own emotional patterns, or their behavior toward their children. Often they are reactive and controlling, without thought or care about how it affects their children.

Other parents I have met have been basically happy but cannot seem to change certain fundamental problems in their lives, which over time wear on them. They might change a little here and there, but they do it only as a band-aid approach.

Some parents are continually growing and responding to their own needs and to the needs of their children. Yet, these parents are in the minority.

The obvious question is this: Why do so few people change, when it is such an essential part of growing as a human being, of becoming an adult, and of learning how to love? The answer is that change, especially at an emotional level, where all true change has to occur, is complex and often frightening. Without guidance and support, change can be extremely difficult.

Change Can Be Difficult

For most people, change can be difficult and challenging. How many of us have had the same habits, the same reactions, and the same manner of relating to certain people—mothers, fathers, spouses, friends, children—for years?

Where did you learn your reactions and habits? How many of them were learned early on in your childhood and teen years? To suddenly change them is far more complex than it looks, particularly if they are based upon past anger, hurt, fear, pain, or shame—which so many of your patterns of behavior are. Your reactions and habits are complex, yet the very nature of change requires you to explore and learn about them, no matter how complex or uncomfortable that may be.

For example, what if the need to control is one of your patterns of behavior? Perhaps this pattern was something you developed as a teen to survive an overbearing and controlling parent. After years of acting out this control pattern, it has become a part of your personality, an unconscious, automatic reaction. Changing it requires that you first start with honesty—to acknowledge you are controlling—which controlling people are reluctant to do. It threatens their control. Then you have to look at when and how you are controlling. And finally, you need a willingness and a determination to learn how to relate differently to people. This process takes time and commitment. It is a very loving and worthwhile choice to change the controlling aspects of yourself, because controlling is the opposite of loving. Yet, how many of us are reluctant to even consider going through this kind of process?

In addition to the complexity of change, how many of us are just plain scared of change because it might rock the boat of our life? How many of us are frightened to admit our faults and mistakes—scared of our hidden shame about our behavior, afraid of being judged, rejected, and humiliated?

Yet, if you want to change you have to deal with the complexities of your patterns as well as your fears. If you avoid looking at your patterns, reactions, and fears, you can easily become entrenched in them, unable to change, even if you know you are being hurtful to yourself and those you love. Sadly, our patterns and habits of behavior can often become more important to us than the people in our lives:

I once met a father who unmercifully and continually pushed his young athletic son to succeed. He began putting on the pressure when his son was only six or seven. "You have the talent. You can be the best! You *will* be the best!" he would say. As it turned out, he did to his son what his father had done to him. His demands, his rage, his shaming of his son when he failed, his need for perfection, were all patterns of behavior his father had acted out on him.

Why did he do these very same things, knowing what it had done to him? He was trying to vent all the pent-up hurt, hate, and rage he was carrying around inside himself. He was passing down his own sense of shame that his father had passed down to him.

His wife continually tried to get him to stop, to change his behavior. He ignored her. His friends told him, "Ease up! You are pressuring your son too much." He tightened the screws on his son even more, seemingly in defiance of others' advice—no one was going to tell him how to raise his boy!

When his son finally rebelled in rage and anger and pain and hate, quitting sports forever to spite his father and withdrawing from the relationship, his father responded. However, he did not respond by learning anything from the experience and changing his behavior. Rather, he shifted his punishing behavior over to his younger son.

I met the younger son, who was fifteen. His coach told me, with a sad shake of his head, that he was already beginning to crack under the weight of his father's behavior. He felt sure the father would end up losing this son also. It was only a matter of time.

Changing yourself is challenging, yet if you sincerely want to grow, to learn about yourself, to love more deeply, to become a better parent, you must be willing to change. You have to muster up the courage to ask yourself who you are, how your life is going, and what the true nature of your relationships are, no matter how frightening the answers may be.

If you are willing to change you can heal your past pains, deal effectively with your patterns of behavior, and continually learn to love on ever-deepening levels.

Changing yourself has another great benefit. Your willingness to change allows your children to see a role model of what a true adult is, as opposed to a "grown-up"—one acting as an adult but with behavior rooted in patterns established in childhood and adolescence. A true adult is always willing to change when appropriate. And by doing so you are teaching your children that no one is perfect, that change is a necessary part of a healthy life. You are also teaching them what individuality, choice, and responsibility are all about.

Change can be difficult and uncomfortable for the many reasons suggested—and for other reasons you can probably offer. Yet, there are two significant reasons that can motivate you to want to change, even though it may be uncomfortable. Each of these reasons can stand alone, but they also work quite well together.

The first reason to change is a desire to have a different, healthier, and more supportive emotional impact on your children.

The second reason for change is simply because you love your children enough to not want to pass down to them your own negative emotional patterns.

Paying Attention to Your Emotional Impact

The definition of the word *impact* is, "the force of impression of one thing on another." In emotional terms, one's "impact" is created by behavior and all that it entails—words, tone of voice, looks, physical stance, moods, warmth or lack of it, outbursts, silence, touch, tenderness, understanding, expectations, approval, judgment, rejection, and more.

As a parent, you *always* have an emotional impact upon your children—

negatively or positively. It is impossible to have a neutral impact. Being willing to pay attention to your impact, with the intent to change if you see that it is not as loving as it could be, is a part of a parent's responsibility.

This may sound like a simple thing to do, yet one of the biggest hurdles parents face is in knowing what their emotional impact upon their children actually is.

One immediate problem is that it is difficult to always know what your children are experiencing. If you ask them what they are feeling, sometimes they will tell you; much of the time they will not. They may be afraid you will not listen to them, or that you will find fault with them. If they are adolescents they may not want to talk to you about their feelings, or they may feel too emotionally confused to know what they are really feeling. Frequently, adolescents will not be truthful, which is often their way of avoiding having to deal with their feelings. Whatever the reason, often you may have to use your own observations to sense what your children are actually feeling.

What will be helpful when sensing what your children are feeling is to always keep in mind that they are young and without experience in life. They do not have the wherewithal to recognize or understand that many things you may do, say, or feel have nothing to do with them. They see everything in personal terms—how it affects them—which only magnifies the significance of everything you do. How you act, what you say—and *how* you say it— the way you relate to your spouse, how hard you work, the struggle in your life, how you deal—or do not deal—with your emotions, all have a definite impact upon your children. The bottom line is that it is up to you to monitor—to be responsible for—your emotional impact upon your children.

Though this is a challenging task, there are many ways to do it. The key lies in paying attention to how your children are feeling and behaving when you relate to them—and then talking to them about what you see. You need to try to find out if they are reacting to something you have said or done, or if they are afraid of you in some way.

Pay attention to how they feel and act. You might be thinking, "I already do that." If you do, that is great. But there is always more to learn about how a child or adolescent feels and thinks.

One of the best ways to be aware of your emotional impact is to ask your children how they feel about how you treat them. Even if they will not talk back to you, or they act like everything is fine, if something seems amiss to you, it is important to ask them how they are feeling. At the very least they will always have the opportunity to voice their feelings—and they will know you care about what they are feeling.

Beyond talking to your children, you can ask yourself, "Did, or does, my behavior cause a negative impact? Do I need to change something?" If you do not know the answer to these questions, ask your spouse for his or her insights. If you can, ask your children about specific actions of yours that may have affected them. Sometimes they might surprise you with their willingness to talk about their feelings.

The Fear of Being a "Bad Parent"

A significant block that I see in parents who are unwilling to question and reflect honestly on their emotional impact is their fear that they might be "bad parents" if they discover negative behavior. These parents usually see what they want to see about their impact, regardless of how their children, or others, feel about it.

Often, I find that these same parents are determined to be better parents than their own were to them. They intend to give their children all the opportunities they never had—and they claim that they are not going to make the same mistakes their parents did. They are so afraid of being "bad parents" that they are frightened to look honestly at their own behavior.

If told by a coach, myself, or another parent, that they are pressuring their kids, they often become defensive, unwilling to hear any feedback. If you find yourself becoming defensive when something is pointed out to you, take the time to look at that something in detail—without the judgment that you might be a bad parent if it is true. It will take courage to look honestly at your behavior if you are the type who judges yourself harshly for making mistakes with your children. Yet, by the very act of looking at your own impact upon your children, you are demonstrating how loving a parent you really are.

Letting Love Be Your Motivation to Change

The greatest motivation for wanting to change your emotional impact is love. Ultimately, love is the granddaddy of all motivations for change. If you ever have a doubt, all you have to do is to remind yourself that your son or daughter has only one father or mother in this world—you. And they desperately need your love. You are the one they learn from and look up to. You are their role model. You are the one they ask for advice. And no matter how arrogant they might act, no matter how much they might complain and feel sorry for themselves, no matter how much they might take you for granted, they still need you.

As children grow older, parents have to allow for the inevitable changes. Young children become adolescents, who think, feel, and act differently than they did as 6-year-olds.

Compromising, discussing, listening, paying attention to mutual needs, talking to one another about feelings, learning responsibilities—are all part of a healthy family. They form the cornerstone for healthy, loving relationships.

Without the space for these things, what would happen to your family? Look around. How many families have become battlegrounds?

You are the keeper of the love—you are the parent. You are the one who needs to nurture, protect, and provide. And it is your willingness to love enough to change that can give your children the positive love they so need.

CHAPTER 7

Learning to Be a More Loving Parent

The question could be asked, perhaps needs to be asked: What does loving a son or daughter look like? What are the components of loving someone? What is it based upon? How do we really know when we are or are not being loving? If we do not know what loving looks like, how will we know if we are loving?

Love without Consciousness

Though there are many parents who are aware of how to love, an extraordinary number of parents are blinded—by past pains, emotional suppression, and distorted views of love—from seeing how unconscious they are in the way they love. They are unaware of their constricting emotional patterns, or refuse to even consider that they might have them, and they make sweeping assumptions about the impact they are having upon their children. These parents have little awareness as to whether they are being loving toward their children. They see and believe what they want, no matter what contradicting feedback they might get. Many just assume they are right, being too frightened to even question themselves for fear they might find out something they do not want to see:

A 16-year-old athlete approached me at a big competition and asked if we could talk. He was so emotionally pent-up, he looked as if he were about to burst. His parents were going to be at the competition.

"I asked them not to come!" he said. "They always do this! They won't let me have my own life!"

He said he had asked them not to come, that he wanted to be just with his team on this particular trip. It was the last trip of the season. They said they understood; they would not come. A half hour before the competition, without warning, they showed up, all smiles.

The boy was so angry while he was relating this to me that he could barely speak. For three years he had been asking his parents not to come to certain competitions. He felt less pressure to perform if they were not there, or sometimes he just wanted to be with the team. And for three years, he said, they came to those competitions, completely disregarding his wishes or concerns. They always acted as if the conversation about their not coming had never happened. He would remind them of the conversation, of his asking them not to come—of their agreeing. They would laugh and say, "Oh, yeah, we know, but we decided we wanted to come and see you. We love you."

They could not understand what their total disregard of his wishes did to him, how unloving it was. He felt controlled, ignored, and devalued. And every time they came to a competition unannounced and unwanted, his anger and rage built up a little more. When he spoke with me, he was so pent-up with emotion that he was barely able to speak without screaming. As he spit his words out, he paced, clenching his fists and jaw continually.

His parents had no idea what their emotional impact was on him. They just smiled and told him how much they loved him.

They never seemed to notice how angry he became and how poorly he performed whenever they came unannounced. And they could not understand why he said he could not talk to them.

It is not a fault to be emotionally unconscious, but there are direct consequences for children. The unconscious parent does not know they are being unloving. They are too unaware of their actions—and their children's feelings.

Becoming More Conscious of How You Love

Though you can be unaware, perhaps afraid to change—frightened of "rocking the boat" or of what you might find if you look too closely—deep within you there *is* a part that knows how to love. That part is your soul: the heart of who you are. The problem and challenge you face is that the loving part of you can be easily clouded or distorted by a number of incidents as you live your daily life, particularly when you are young. Your responsibility as an adult and as a parent is to look for and become conscious of your clouding and distortions so you can then heal and change yourself. As you heal and change, you will automatically become more conscious of how you love.

In your search for awareness, perhaps the first place to start is to realize that you were taught how to love, principally by how your mother and father, family members, and other authority figures treated you. You also picked up beliefs about love from movies, books, friends, locker-room talk, and all sorts of other places.

While you will have some awareness of how to love, many of your beliefs about love may be faulty. To a certain extent they have to be. Many of your decisions about love were made when you were a child and adolescent, with little experience or wisdom in life, especially about how to love. In addition, you were particularly vulnerable to your environment. What if you were raised by a parent who knew little about loving? How many of your perceptions about love during childhood and adolescence had more fantasy to them than truth? There are also memories of painful experiences associated with love. Some were experienced through family members, while others were created by hurtful friendships and failed, romantic relationships that you witnessed or experienced. There may also have been major incidents, such as death, divorce, or something else as serious. All of these incidents and life experiences added together will color the nature of loving, without your even being aware of it.

Despite the distortion of beliefs and your painful memories about love, you can grow beyond your past and learn to love in a conscious and positive way. In fact, learning to love beyond your past difficulties and pains is a necessary step in maturing into an emotionally responsible adult—and parent.

Loving consciously is based upon adult values, not child or adolescent perceptions, fears, and insecurities. This kind of loving takes time to learn and a willingness to clear up your unhealthy perceptions surrounding love. It also requires a responsibility to heal whatever pain you may be carrying that is associated with past experiences of love. Pain will always compromise your perceptions of loving, never allowing you to be free of your past.

Loving consciously also takes a certain degree of emotional depth. You develop this through your experiences in life, which include your joys, loves, laughter, fun, and the many other positive times in your life. It also includes healing and coming to terms with your losses, pains, hurts, angers, and other such emotions.

To consciously love, you need to be willing to feel and express your emotions. There are many grown-ups who are so emotionally out of touch that they feel very little. Often, everyone is aware of it but them.

The "strong silent types," for example—the ones who never express their emotions—do not have true mastery over their feelings. Not expressing one's emotions most often comes from the fear of dealing with deeper feelings—being vulnerable—and an unwillingness to let anyone come too close. Fear of losing control, rather than an abundance of strength, is the real motivation for the silent types.

Expressing how you feel responsibly is part of being an adult and a parent, and it is essential to consciously loving. Just the simple act of telling someone "I love you"—not just the words, but with genuine feeling—on a regular basis is a fundamental part of consciously loving. Your willingness to communicate your feelings is necessary to reassure those you love. Just look at how often children need to be reminded that they are loved.

Love is an unending subject by nature, and none of us will ever know all there is to know about it. Yet, there are certain ways you can consciously act that will produce the feeling of being loved. Knowing and practicing these actions of love can help you learn how to be more conscious of your loving.

Loving Actions

The term *loving* has a different meaning than the word *love*. *Love* describes a feeling. *Loving* describes a mode of behavior, the way one acts. While you may love someone, that does not mean you always act loving toward them. Love is demonstrated through "loving actions," which are meant to produce the feeling of being loved.

These actions are specific and will work for anyone. You will recognize all of them; they are not new. Each of the actions is meant to produce a feeling in the person you are loving.

It is important to recognize that the actions of loving another are the very same actions used for loving yourself. The more you are willing to love yourself, the more you will understand and know how to love someone else.

A List of Loving Actions

These actions and the following list of feelings they elicit will be described in terms of loving another. Simply apply the same definitions to loving yourself.

1. **Giving:** Love, time, tenderness, understanding, patience, money, support—the list could go on for pages. Giving because you want to, not giving to get something in return. Giving because it is needed. Giving because it makes the person you love feel good.
2. **Responding to another's needs:** Emotionally, spiritually, mentally, and physically—whatever their needs may be (to be understood, to feel safe, to be communicated with, to be cared for, etc.).
3. **Respecting:** Another's emotional nature. Always treating another's feelings as if they are as important as your own—because they are. Caring enough to understand and relate to what that person is feeling, not just to what they are thinking, is respecting him or her.
4. **Knowing:** A person's vulnerabilities, strengths, and emotional needs will help you understand how to respect and respond to him or her.

Knowing takes the most patience, understanding, and love. You have to be willing to try and see life through their eyes, their emotions, and their needs.

5. **Committing:** To another, to his or her welfare and happiness. Committing in a way that engenders trust. Being there for that person no matter what.

6. **Having humility:** To always know that a person can be more, learn more, and grow more, but without judging his or her faults. Seeing his or her beauty, goodness, potential, and lovability, no matter how much he or she fails.

7. **Caring:** In your actions, communication, and thoughts. Demonstrating you care in a such a way that another knows it. Showing concern for another's needs. Being considerate.

When loving yourself, do all these actions for your own benefit. Give to yourself, respond to your own needs, respect your feelings by letting yourself feel them, know yourself, be committed to yourself, have humility for yourself, and act in a caring manner toward yourself.

Feelings That Loving Actions Are Meant to Produce

These feelings are what you would feel when you are being loved by another.

1. **Increased Sense of Security of Being Loved:** Knowing your emotional needs are understood and respected. Knowing another is committed to you—emotionally and physically. Being reassured whenever you are frightened over a potential loss of love or support.

2. **Vulnerability and Honesty:** An atmosphere in which you can be emotionally open. You feel free to tell the truth. Not feeling wrong or judged when you are being honest, even if another may feel uncomfortable with what you are saying. You feel a sense of closeness.

3. **Intimacy and Caring:** Being cared for, considered, appreciated, understood. Another is sensitive to your needs and concerns. There is an emotional openness and a sense of tenderness, gentleness, closeness, vulnerability, and trust.

4. **Being Known:** Feeling appreciated for who you are. There is a recognition of your vulnerabilities, inadequacies, and emotional pains, without judgment.

5. **Safety and Security:** Free from emotional or physical threat. You feel another's commitment and loyalty. You do not fear abandonment or betrayal. You can talk honestly about your emotions.

6. **Pleasure:** The delight and enjoyment of another's love, company,

consideration, understanding, patience, laughter, conversation, and all the other things you cherish about another.

7. **Trust:** You can rely upon another. Another will hold your secrets dear and in confidence, and will not use them against you. The sense that you can be vulnerable without fear. Knowing another will never intentionally hurt you. Knowing that if you make a mistake, you will not be judged or rejected.

These lists—loving actions and their corresponding feelings—are fundamental components of loving someone. They are not meant to be complete lists, but they offer a foundation for learning how to consciously love your children (as well as yourself, your spouse, or anyone else). You can add whatever you want from the lists to what you already know about loving.

Before you do anything else though, take the time to reflect upon these lists. They are much more than words and definitions. Go below the surface. Be willing to be honest with yourself about how consciously you are loving.

Ask yourself several questions:

❏ What actions am I already doing?
❏ How often am I being loving?
❏ At what times am I most loving, least loving?
❏ Do I reward performance with love?
❏ What do I need to do more?
❏ What can I improve upon?
❏ What actions am I not doing, and how is this affecting my children?

And with a deeper, perhaps more penetrating look, ask yourself these questions.

❏ Do I control sometimes rather than love?
❏ Does it have to be my way all the time, and how does this attitude affect my children?
❏ Do I have open discussions with my children, or is it mainly me telling them how it is going to be?
❏ Do I talk openly about my feelings with my children?
❏ Am I approachable and emotionally safe to talk to?
❏ Do I seek my children out when they have emotional problems?
❏ Do I usually look at my children's achievements first—and their feelings second?
❏ Do I tell my children how much I love them? How often?

If you want to know how your children feel about some of these questions, ask them. And ask them if they would like to be spoken to or treated differently. You may not be able to do everything they request. Some of it may be unreasonable, but you might be able to change certain things that are important to them. Your willingness to change will mean a lot to them. It will also demonstrate that you understand them and are willing to recognize their needs, which is so important to consciously loving them.

Though these actions of loving are not difficult to learn, some people may have certain blocks in their emotional past that prevent them from being vulnerable enough to let themselves love—or be loved—to any great degree. If you are one of these people, you will be more able to open up to the whole issue of love if you are willing to do some healing work. If you have not done any work on yourself, or if you have not done enough to heal yet, you might consider using the two reasons to change—your emotional impact and your love for your children—as new and stronger motivations to now do what is needed to heal yourself. More will be said about these issues later in the book.

Your Emotions

CHAPTER 8

The Complexity
of Emotions

There is an assumption in our society that certain emotions are considered "positive"—love, laughter, joy, happiness—while others are looked upon as being "negative"—fear, hate, anger, hurt. While these are generally accepted perceptions, in fact they are far from being true, and they are very misleading.

Let us start with the very concept of positive and negative emotions. That is all it is—a concept. There are no inherently "positive" or "negative" emotions. Rather, *all* emotions—when expressed responsibly, when not used to hurt anyone, are positive and expanding, just as *all* emotions, including love, when suppressed and stuffed down inside of us become negative and constricting.

We relate to our world through all of our emotions, not just some of them. How we feel about someone or something determines the nature of that relationship. Intense emotions, from love and joy to anger and hurt, all have value. They give our relationships understanding, meaning, and a wide dimension of experience. If we decide that some emotions are less positive than others, we often end up wanting to deny—to refrain from feeling—the so-called negative emotions, thinking something is wrong with us unless we do.

The Importance of Feeling

Emotions are given to all of us. We are meant to feel them; that is why we have them. That is what makes us human. It could be said that the more intensely we feel, the more alive, happy, and healthy we are. And perhaps most important, the more deeply—intensely—we feel our emotions, the more understanding, loving, and patient we become.

On the other hand, if we deny or stay on the surface with our emotions, we end up limiting our ability to connect with and relate to the most important people in our lives—our friends and families. If we deny our feelings too much, we can reach a point where our lives and relationships become shallow and empty, ultimately without meaning or connection.

Most of us just assume that we feel our feelings. We do not look too closely at which emotions we feel—or avoid—most often, how reactive we are in specific situations, or how expressive—or suppressive—we really are.

Very few of us choose to learn about and explore our emotional self unless we are forced to, usually by a crisis of some kind. It is too scary. We are used to avoiding uncomfortable or painful feelings; we do not usually go searching for them. This is what we learned growing up. This is how we protected ourselves from pain and discomfort. It became a habit that we have forgotten we have.

This does not mean we do not feel at all. Rather, out of habit, we have limited how deeply we are willing to feel, for fear of what we might find.

Whether we currently feel deeply or only superficially, we can always learn to feel *more* deeply with *more* emotional awareness and sensitivity.

The Cost of Avoiding Feelings

Our emotions are the lifelines to everything in our lives. Feeling them provides us with depth, fulfillment, and the sense of being alive. If we suppress or deny our emotions—to any extent—there is a cost. The greater the suppression or denial, the greater the cost.

All of our emotions are like powerful sources of live energy, each one carrying its own unique "electromagnetic charge." This charge can be felt—and even recorded.

Lie detector tests that are used by law enforcement agencies demonstrate this. When someone is lying, he or she feels fear, which causes a physical charge of energy to surge through their bodies. This charge is what the lie detector's receptors pick up.

We can feel these emotional surges of energy. That is why emotions are called feelings—because we feel them. When we genuinely feel an emotion, we are in essence spending—using up, you could say—its charge. The feeling essentially passes through us, giving us a specific experience, which is unique to each emotion. After a feeling has been experienced, we now can fully feel the next emotion that comes along.

If we try to suppress or avoid emotions such as pain, anger, and hurt because they are uncomfortable, painful, or, in our minds, negative, the charge these emotions carry becomes trapped inside of us. If we continue to suppress and avoid, we only increase the energy and power of this charge. A charge that becomes too built-up constricts the natural flow of energy that the expression of our emotions gives us. By not feeling our emotions, we create pent-up charges of energy that eventually have very draining and damaging effects upon our lives, especially our relationships.

Take a look at how you feel when you become pent-up with emotion. How edgy do you become? How understanding and loving do you feel? How reactive and angry do you become at the smallest things? How often do you end up feeling depressed, not knowing why?

The more we are willing to feel our emotions—whether they are comfortable or not—the more we allow their energy to flow through us. In this way, we prevent debilitating charges of energy from becoming trapped inside of us. We can experience our lives—and relationships—with greater richness and deeper meaning.

The "Numbed Out" Parent

If you avoid feeling a particular emotion for any length of time, you can end up not even knowing it is there, no matter how many people might tell you otherwise. You become "numb"—detached and insensitive—to what you are feeling deeper inside of you. With the additional emotional challenges in life that parenthood offers, it can be relatively easy to get in the habit of numbing yourself just to get through a given day.

The problem that numbing one's self causes is that it is like taking a warm bath. There is a certain seduction to it—warm baths are comfortable. You do not have to think about, feel, or deal with anything that you do not want to. All you have to do is stay in the false comfort of the warm water. Unless you consciously change how you respond to your feelings—stop the habit of numbing yourself—no matter how uncomfortable those feelings might be, you will only increase your numbness, making it more difficult to emotionally connect with those around you. Children will be the most sensitive to, and the most hurt by, the disconnection that numbness creates in relationships.

There is a multitude of mothers and fathers who do not express their emotions very easily—with each other or with their children. Most often these parents, because they are emotionally suppressed, are not even aware they are numbed out to many of their feelings.

Parents who have lost touch with their emotions act in many different ways: overly compliant, overprotective, constantly talking, dominating, bitingly sarcastic, punishing, and humiliating. These parents are not consciously dealing with specific emotions. Instead they are playing them out through their behavior.

Perhaps one of the most recognized types of behavior that shows up in youth sports is the parent who "blows up." These parents are suppressed and numbed out to their own anger, shame, and rage—and, unfortunately, to the emotional impact it has upon their children. They are unaware that being insensitive to an emotion does not keep that emotion from bursting out at others. They usually do not even see their blow-ups as being unusual or hurtful.

Their children, on the other hand, are very aware of their parents' impact upon them. Most are afraid to share their feelings with their parents. Repeated experiences of being yelled at, made to feel small, or being ignored or misunderstood have been too painful.

One example of this type of parent, a father, and the effect he had upon his daughter, comes to mind:

The girl was a talented young athlete, adept in two different sports. During the seminar she was attentive and curious, seemingly at ease. At a certain point, she raised her hand, wanting to ask a question. Her demeanor changed immediately when she began speaking.

"I compete in two different sports," she began. "I really enjoy both of them, and I have close friends on both teams. My father says I have to choose to compete in only one sport at the end of this season. He says I can't excel in either sport if I continue to do both at the same time. I know that's probably true, but I don't want to stop doing either one. I won't be able to see my friends anymore." At that point her composure broke. Small tears began to run down her cheeks. She bit her lip and looked down.

"Losing your friends is no small thing," I said gently.

She nodded.

"It is true that it is easier to focus on just one sport," I continued. "Any coach can tell you that. And when you reach a certain age it is normal for most serious athletes to decide which sport they want to focus on."

She nodded again.

"But it is also true that some athletes do compete in two sports," I added. "I know many of them. They find coaches that allow them to do that and continue competing, often all the way through college. The idea of sports is to have fun—as well as to try and do your best," I continued. "If having fun for you is competing in both, what is wrong with that? And who is to say that you cannot excel doing both?"

"I would really like to continue competing on both teams, but my father will never let me," she said, shaking her head.

"Have you told him how important it is for you to compete in both sports?" I asked. "Have you acknowledged that it may be difficult to achieve your best in either one, but you would like to try because you enjoy both sports too much to give one up?"

She began shaking her head from side to side. "I can't disagree with my father. It is not allowed," she blurted out.

"You cannot disagree with your father? Ever?"

"No," she repeated, shaking her head even more vigorously.

"What do you mean it is not allowed?"

She looked down at the ground and began to cry, then to sob. Through her hands, which were covering her face, she said, "He has told me not to disagree with him—he knows what is best for me. He yells at me if I ever try to disagree. His yelling scares me so much—it's so loud. I never disagree with him anymore—ever."

"How long has it been this way?" I asked.

"As long as I can remember," she answered.

"Would it help if I spoke to him about your competing in both sports?"

"No! Please don't! He can't know I talked to you about him. He'll get so angry at me. Please, please, don't talk to him," she pleaded.

"Don't worry," I told her. "I will not speak to him. It was only a suggestion."

We continued speaking, but her only choice, being as things were with her father, was to quit one sport, and she could still not bear the thought of that.

Later on, I spoke to the coach. His experience was the same as the girl's. He said the father was very controlling, explosive, and had to be right about everything. The girl was, in the coach's words, "Scared to death of him."

Though most of you may not act like this father, to whatever degree you avoid your feelings—by numbing yourself—your children will know it. And they will feel the effects of it.

Emotionally closed and numbed-out parents have little chance of ever really understanding or even seeing their children's needs. Eventually, they can and usually do become alienated from their own children. And typically, they never understand why, often blaming their children for the problem.

The Value of Expressing Yourself

Expressing your feelings to your spouse and children is one of the healthiest and most valuable habits you can practice—both for you and for them. You are establishing an atmosphere that teaches your children, by demonstration, how to express and value their emotions. You are opening up channels of communication with your children that will prove invaluable for the rest of their lives. You are telling your children that feelings matter, that *their* feelings matter. You are creating an atmosphere of intimacy and connection within your family. And you are valuing your children's emotional selves, which is a very positive and caring way of loving them.

Your children are young athletes, facing the competitive nature of sports, which is fraught with the unexpected. Their need for emotional security is great. Anything you do that can make it easier for them to express their feelings is of great value, for it increases their personal sense of security.

You—the parent—set the example for your children. You are the only one who can establish and maintain an emotionally open and secure environment. Your children are not old or mature enough to do it on their own. If you cannot or will not open up and talk about your own feelings, your children will not be free to open up and talk about theirs. Under these circumstances, it is very easy for a child and parent to end up feeling cut off from each other.

Because roadblocks to communicating feelings are quite normal in any family, it is necessary that you take the lead in maintaining a stable and open environment. This way you have the opportunity to establish a secure atmosphere, as well as to help your children continually learn to express themselves in a healthy and productive way.

Expressing our feelings, particularly between parents and children, offers far more benefits to us than suppressing them. Yet how many of us actually do it?

Consider these questions.

❒ Have you ever taken the time to honestly look at your comfort level with your own feelings?
❒ How expressive are you? (If you do not know, ask your friends.)
❒ Are you comfortable with only certain feelings, while avoiding others?
❒ How much emotion do you hold inside of you?
❒ Do you blow up very often?
❒ Do you try to feel only "positive" emotions?
❒ When was the last time you felt the depth of your anger, hurt, fear, love, happiness, joy?
❒ How open were your parents with their emotions when you were growing up?
❒ How did the way your parents expressed themselves influence the way you express yourself?
❒ How often did you talk to your father about your feelings? Your mother?
❒ Are you following in your parents' emotional footsteps in any way?

If you really want to find out how expressive you are, ask the people closest to you—your spouse, your kids, your friends—how they see you. It might be a sobering experience, if you believe you are very expressive, to find out they see you differently. And then again, you may not have been giving yourself credit for how open you really are, how emotionally secure others feel around you. Either way, it can only help you learn more about yourself.

Unfortunately, there are public perceptions and learned modes of behavior that can make the open expression of feelings a difficult thing for some of us to do.

How often do you hear someone apologize for crying in front of others—for "becoming emotional"? How many are threatened by someone who openly expresses deeply felt emotion? How many men are afraid of being labeled "weak" if they show tears or hurt of any kind?

Those who believe they are being expressive because they blow up on a regular basis—a commonly held perception by many—might want to reconsider that belief. There is a distinct difference between expressing feelings and "exploding." If we would just express our feelings as we feel them and do so in an appropriate manner, we would not create such a buildup of emotion. This would eliminate our need to emotionally explode.

There are a multitude of reasons you can find for not expressing yourself: public perceptions, uncomfortable feelings, fear of your emotions, misconceptions of masculinity. Unless you let them, none of them can stop you from growing beyond your limitations of expression if you really want to change.

Expressing your emotions is essential if you want to feel closely connected to others, and it is absolutely necessary in creating healthy relationships, especially between children and parents.

Becoming a More Open Parent

So how do you begin—or further—the process of becoming more comfortable and open in expressing yourself?

1. Begin with a willingness to change—deciding that whatever your current ability to express yourself, there is always more to learn.
2. Commit to a process of learning how to become more open and expressive—even if it is frightening, even if there is every excuse in the world not to do it.
3. Take time—even if it is only ten minutes a day or every other day—to follow through and do the "work." The work is whatever you need to pay attention to now—releasing your emotions on a deeper level, changing certain patterns of negative behavior, expressing your feelings to a son or daughter, reading a book to learn something about yourself, etc.

4. Allow room for mistakes. When you make a mistake—and you will—
you can forgive yourself and try again.

It is helpful in any process of growth to understand that you have a certain resistance to change, particularly when it deals with your emotions. You are used to your comfort zone, your ways of protecting yourself, your self-images. Who wants to find out that how they have always seen themselves has been distorted and is very different from how they really are?

It can be frightening to examine how you feel and why you do or do not express yourself. You are looking at an unknown. Yet once you begin growing and changing, it becomes easier. The rewards have such far-reaching effects upon you and those you love, you will wonder why you waited so long to grow past your previous boundaries.

Raising and providing for a family—especially an athletic one—takes a lot of time and energy. Many parents will never find the time or want to give any effort to learning how to become more expressive and open, even though the benefits are great. And then there are those parents who consider their ability to express themselves so valuable to their relationship with their children that they will always manage to find a way to learn more about it.

Ultimately, you do not have to do anything about the level of your emotional awareness and expression. It is a matter of preference. What kind of parent do you want to be?

CHAPTER 9

Taking Charge
of Your
Emotions

Taking charge of your emotions means that you are willing to take responsibility for your feelings *and* their impact upon other's, especially your children. It also means you are willing to take charge of how others treat you by letting them know what their impact is on you—both negative *and* positive. And it means you are willing to resolve old issues with your parents or anyone else when these issues still negatively affect your life today. If you will not take charge of your emotions, you will become imprisoned by them.

The problem is, how many of us have been taught how to deal effectively and responsibly with our emotions? The answer is, few of us. In traditional society, there are still many who feel that in asking for help to understand how and why they feel the way they do, they are somehow admitting that there is something wrong with them. For many, even looking at how they themselves really feel about something is risking too much. What if they see something they do not like—then what do they do?

Yet, taking charge of your emotions is one of the most valuable, self esteem-enhancing, and respectful things you can do, for it provides greater emotional security for you and your children. You become more trustworthy and more emotionally reliable.

In essence, when you take charge of your emotions, you take charge of your life.

The Magic of Healing

The magical aspect of taking charge of your emotions is that each time you release and heal an emotional constriction within yourself, that *one* change positively affects your entire being. That is because all your emotions, constricting and expanding, are linked together, existing in the space of your consciousness.

If you are constricted, with anger say, over a specific incident that happened to you, no matter when that anger occurred, *all* your emotions are constricted to some extent until that original constriction is released and healed. The more constricted any emotion becomes, the greater it affects all your other emotions. This is why, for example, powerfully constricting emotions like shame and grief can have lifetime effects upon people unless they are healed.

On the other hand, the more you release *any* constricted emotion, the more *all* other emotions in your consciousness will be freer of the constricting energy around them. This is why someone can heal an emotional incident in their lives that holds deep pain and have their lives turn around in a remarkably positive way, often within just hours, days, or weeks.

Parents, as well as young, college, and pro athletes, have been amazed by how much better they have felt by spending just twenty minutes appropriately expressing their anger. By writing down on paper or expressing in a visualization the anger they felt about an incident, they have released the anger's energy and released themselves from its hold.

The magic of healing by releasing pent-up emotions can profoundly affect your life. Every time you release a suppressed emotion, a pain, a debilitating pattern, or a constricted way of seeing life, you reclaim a lost part of yourself. You become more of who you really are. You grow.

I know firsthand just how magical—and valuable—taking charge of my emotions is. There was a particular pattern of behavior, a way of reacting to certain emotional situations, that I played out for many years. Its origins were in my childhood and teen years, specifically connected to my relationship with my mother. She had several constricting emotions—and corresponding patterns—that had an indelible impact upon my life. My emotional reactions to her formed the basis of a pattern that I developed to protect myself from her hurtful behavior.

The pattern worked like this. Whenever something unexpected that caused hurt happened in my life—an emotional loss, shame, humiliation, or the feeling of being blamed—I immediately became angry. This reaction emerged particularly in close relationships.

Eventually, I discovered that underneath that anger was fear. Before that discovery, I did not even accept the possibility that I might be afraid, because I did not consciously feel any fear. I believed that if I did not feel something, it did not exist. At that point in my life, I did not have any inkling as to how numb to my feelings I had become.

What I also did not know was that unexpected events always made me feel like my life was out of control—that anything could happen. And as it turned out, this feeling of "loss of control" was the root of my fear.

Fear of what though? At first I really did not know. Yet, as I continued going back in time in visualizations (using the visualization process described later in this section), I discovered several incidents that I had completely forgotten in which I was deeply hurt in my childhood and early adolescence.

During that period of my young life, I had no control over certain recurring painful events with my mother. Living in fear of impending pain became a daily experience. I was scared to death of being out of control—it meant I could not protect myself from my mother's actions and words. Rather than feel my fear, I became angry. Anger was my protection. As long as I was angry, I could avoid feeling the fear that was just beneath it.

Anger became the only feeling with which I was comfortable. Anger was also an aggressive emotion; it gave me a false sense of gaining back the control I felt I was losing. I could fight back with anger.

This use of anger to gain back control became a reactive pattern early on in my life to protect me from the fear of feeling out of control. When I finally recognized this pattern, I began consciously to feel my fear instead of the anger. Eventually, being willing to feel my fear opened the door for me to discover the original painful events from my childhood and teen years. I had completely buried these memories to avoid ever having to feel the pain associated with them.

As I reexperienced those events in my visualizations, feeling the emotions associated with them—fear, hurt, and pain—instead of just the anger, I was able to finally heal and release them. The key in healing them was in *feeling* the emotions I felt then, replaying the scene through as it occurred at age ten, thirteen, or sixteen—until there was no more pain, hurt, or other emotions around the incidents left to feel. Feeling, and releasing, these emotions is what ultimately broke the pattern.

I still have some old reactions left from that pattern, but not the original charged emotions that created them. I can now easily recognize and defuse any anger reaction I might have, knowing I do not have to fear losing control any longer.

Ending this pattern has done wonders for my sense of security, self-esteem, confidence, and my relationship with everyone who is close to me, particularly my wife.

The Debilitating Effects of Shame

Shame has been mentioned earlier in this book, but because of the far-reaching and oftentimes emotionally crippling effects it can have on all of us, the overall issue of shame deserves to be looked at in greater depth.

We all develop some degree of shame, principally during childhood and in our adolescence. Much of it is tied to our relationships with our parents. They are the ones we use to interpret our worth and sense of value. How they act and speak to us, to each other, and to our siblings has great impact upon how we see ourselves.

Parents are not the only source of shame. Siblings, friends, and other authority figures can also contribute.

We can be shamed in various ways, such as through the use of demeaning and hurtful words, slashing tones of voice, continual demands we cannot meet, and various forms of control or domination. Ridicule, constant correction or criticism, blame, rejection, unattainable expectations, and humiliation likewise will cause shame.

There are also many seemingly innocent behaviors that over time will cause shame, such as a father repeatedly talking to his son about following him into his business. After awhile, that son may feel that he cannot say no to his father's plans for him without feeling shameful—that he is an ungrateful son. There are also the struggling parents, whose children feel like they do not have the right to have an easy, comfortable life—how shameful to even consider it after all their parents went through. And then there are the parents who constantly sacrifice for their children. Their children see this and can easily end up feeling deep shame, blaming themselves for ruining their parents' lives. Look how much their parents gave up for them, they think.

The most difficult aspect of shame is how easily it can be hidden. Many people do not realize that the reason they cannot hang up the phone on a constantly self-pitying parent is the childhood shame they still carry. They hate listening to their mother complain, but they would never consider telling her the truth about her actions. That would only hurt her, they say, so instead they complain to everyone else in the family, to all their friends, and to anyone else who will listen, not realizing they are doing just what their mother is doing to them.

The reason why it is so difficult to recognize shame is because it is such an all-encompassing, painful feeling. Who wants to feel that? It is often described as feeling "wrong," "bad," or "not good enough." It is as if something is inherently wrong with you—that you are flawed somehow—which causes you to feel separated from others. And because of this "flaw," and the sense of separation it causes, you are frightened, often terrified, of ever making a mistake. You are sure people will then see your flaw, which will only cause further separation. Because shame can cause such pain, for many, just the word itself can make one shudder.

If we do not heal our shame it will become a part of our everyday life, just like any other suppressed emotion we carry around. And like any other emotion, whether we are aware of it or not, we will communicate it to others around us, particularly to our children.

A typical example that is common in competitive athletics are the parents who always feel disappointed when their children fail to perform up to their expectations. The parents, in one way or another—with a look, a tone of voice, or certain words—let their children know they have failed. Whatever they accomplished, unless it met with dad's or mom's expectations, was not good enough. Oftentimes, this is done during the competitions—in front of other young athletes and their parents. These children always end up feeling like they should be better, more successful, more committed—more something. After awhile, they do not feel good even about their outstanding performances; they just feel more and more pressure to continually live up to their own success.

These children are trapped. If they perform well, they increase the pressure on themselves to continue doing well. If they do not do well, they have to face their parents' judgment and the ensuing feelings of shame that they are "not good enough" in their parents' eyes.

Sadly, unless there is a change, the parents and their children end up playing this pattern out for the rest of their lives—the parents continually reminding their children (even when the "children" are middle aged), in one way or another, that they are "not good enough," and the children usually resenting their parents for their continual judgment.

If you look deeper into this example, you will usually find that the parents of these parents had the same pattern with their fathers or mothers. *They* were the children who were not good enough, and the feelings of shame they developed because of this were then passed down later on to their own children.

The passing down of shame is multigenerational, never ending until someone has the courage to heal it.

Though shame is commonly passed on through family relationships, it is also generated in other significant ways. Violent incidents such as rape, molestation, or physical abuse will most certainly cause great pain and shame.

The questions always asked by victims of rape or abuse are, "Why did this happen to me? What is so wrong with me that I was singled out? Why didn't God protect me?" The conclusion the victims come to, no matter what the explanation, is "There must be something wrong with me—I'm somehow flawed."

After all that has been said about shame, it might seem improbable that there could be a positive side to it. There actually is, but that occurs only after the shame is healed. After healing your shame, you lose your need to be "perfect," because perfectionism is always an attempt to hide shame. You no longer have to be afraid of making mistakes; you recognize that making mistakes is human, not shameful. And you no longer feel flawed, because shame is what made you feel that way in the first place. You also develop a tremendous compassion and empathy for another's shame, because you have understood and healed your own. And because you have released the constricting influence of shame upon your emotions, you greatly increase your capacity to feel more deeply, to love with greater understanding, and to give more freely.

Perhaps the greatest benefit of healing shame is that you will not pass it down to your children.

If you know, or suspect, that you are still carrying unresolved shame, the first step in healing it is to acknowledge that you feel it. Then begin exploring as much as you can the issue of shame so you can understand on a deeper level what it is and how it is affecting you.

Books that can be very helpful are readily available, such as John Bradshaw's *Healing the Shame That Binds You*. You can also seek professional help or work with a group that specifically deals with the healing of shame.

Day-to-Day Feelings

Much has been discussed already about constricted emotions and what their impact can be, yet patterns of behavior are only one place to find constricted emotions. Another significant place to look is the day-to-day emotions we all have, but usually do not take the time to express.

As a parent, especially one of a young athlete, you are called upon to show patience, understanding, compassion, love, and many other qualities. You also need to be a disciplinarian, provider, protector, nurturer, driver, cook, home keeper, cheerleader, advice-giver, and a full-service bank—to name just a few things. Showing and being all these things are in addition to your own personal day-to-day responsibilities, job, and relationship with your spouse.

Do you think that with all of this activity and responsibility you just might, at times, feel hurt, frustrated, fearful, angry, rageful, confused, and any number of other emotions that come up in an ordinary day, week, or month? At the same time, with most of us having a lack of understanding and practice of effectively responding to our emotions, is it any wonder that over time you can frequently end up having a buildup of many different feelings?

In addition, there are other, more significant day-to-day issues that contribute to a buildup of emotion. Such things as conflicts with time schedules, sibling rivalries, difficulty communicating with an adolescent, and disappointments over your children's losses take an emotional toll on parents.

These issues, usually day-to-day in nature, if not dealt with, can become very emotionally charged, often causing major conflicts within families.

When you add up all the day-to-day issues, you are facing a potential source of emotional buildup. You do not have to get rid of all day-to-day issues; many are a natural part of life, especially the life of an athlete's parent. But if you ignore your feelings, you can end up becoming pent-up with a tangle of emotions, not knowing for sure just what you are feeling.

The seduction and challenge with day-to-day issues is that you can get used to going with the flow. You can end up just accepting turmoil, pressure, and charged issues as a way of life—to the point where you do not recognize your true feelings anymore. A lot of parents are overwhelmed with pent-up, day-to-day emotions. They just get by from one day to the next. Most do not know how to respond in an effective manner to their feelings, so they just continue avoiding them. Others have simply stopped caring; their lives have become about struggle and going through the motions. Self-pity and martyrdom have become their way of coping.

Perhaps the most damaging results of pent-up day-to-day emotions are the immediate and long-term effects they can have upon your children. When small, suppressed emotions—particularly frustration and anger—combine with each other and become pent-up, you end up creating an emotional constriction within you—a significant block of charged energy. As with all constrictions, you end up debilitating your normal flow of life energy, your ability to perceive others' feelings accurately, and your own emotional sensitivity and stability. In short, if you allow your day-to-day feelings to build up inside of you you can have a negative influence upon your children and not even be aware of it .

Here is an example of what can happen when "small" suppressed frustrations build up a collective charge over time. How many times have you shared a meal with family or friends and watched two people begin to argue over something, usually an insignificant issue? Suddenly the tone of the conversation escalates. Tension is high. Someone blows up, and everyone becomes quiet, not knowing what to do. If you have ever experienced this or a like situation, especially as a child, you will know firsthand how uncomfortable and frightening it can be.

Bursts of emotion like this are common in many families—I hear about them all the time from young athletes. I cannot even count the number of times young athletes have tried to laugh off or explain away a parent's outbursts by saying, "That's just dad [or mom]." Yet, when questioned more closely, many of these same kids end up talking about how frightened and confused they are, often bursting into tears. Many others try to hide what they are really feeling, but it always shows in their eyes:

Joan raised her hand, not straight up, but sort of halfway up, pointing toward me. Her eyes were filled with sadness, the kind that made me feel sad just looking at her. While I held her gaze, I wondered what had happened to her. No words passed between us, yet tears were already beginning to fill her eyes.

"I work five days a week. I am in all honor classes, with a lot of homework every night. I train six days a week," she began. Then she just shook her head and looked down.

"How old are you, Joan?" I asked.

"Fifteen," she said.

"You can't do all that; it's too much," I said. "Why are you doing so much?"

"I have to."

"Why do you have to? Is someone making you do it?"

"It's my family," she answered. "My father becomes very angry easily. He has always wanted me and my brother to get good grades—all A's. My brother never has done quite that well. Every time his report card comes home my father goes berserk. I can't stand it when he yells. It's so scary. I don't know what he might do."

"What does he usually do?" I asked.

"He suddenly blows up. We never see it coming. He screams at my brother, me, and my mother. Then he starts throwing things like pans and our toaster and bowls—big heavy things—everywhere. We all get under the dining room table as fast as we can so we won't be hit by anything. The worst part is that when he is done screaming and throwing things, he suddenly acts like nothing ever happened. There's stuff smashed, laying all over the house, and he asks us how our day has gone.

"Lately my father has been talking of divorce. He is blaming himself for my brother's failures," she said. "'Why should we stay as a family if we can't raise our kids right?' he is saying. And my brother is getting lower grades all the time.

"I have to make up for my brother," she added. "I can't be another disappointment to my father. If I don't, I'm afraid my family will break up."

Her tears, which she had been blinking back while she was speaking, were now rolling down her cheeks.

"So all this work, the training, the honor classes, this is to show how much you can achieve so your father will feel like he is a successful parent?" I asked.

"Yes."

"Do you think your only value as a person is based on what you achieve, that achievement is all a parent can look to as the measurement of a child?" I asked. "Do you think you have nothing else to offer?"

She just looked at me, saying nothing.

Her teammates, who were sitting on the floor as she was, had been listening to our conversation in silence. But while we were speaking, several girls had

slowly moved closer and closer to her until four of them had formed a tight cir-
cle around her. Two had reached out and were touching her arm.

"There are four girls sitting rather close to you who weren't there when we
began speaking. Why do you think they are there now?" I asked.

She shook her head. "I don't know."

One of the girls put her arms around her and gently embraced her.

"They do," I said. "Why don't some of you tell Joan what she doesn't know
yet."

Several hands went up immediately—from all over the room—from girls and
boys.

"I won't call on any of you," I said. "Just talk to her in your own way."

"You are my closest friend," one began. "I don't care what you achieve—or
don't. It never has and never will affect our friendship."

"You are our leader, Joan," another added. "We would not be the same team
without you—I would not be here if it weren't for you. You are always smiling
and laughing. It makes me smile and laugh. It makes everything seem easier."

"You have always been there for me," one told her. "I can count on you more
than anyone but my parents."

"You have such courage. You never back down from a challenge," one of the
girls next to her said. "It amazes me. And I think to myself, 'If Joan can do it, I
can do it.'"

Comment after comment continued to speak of how positively she affected
others, through her friendship, her kindness, her warm smile and leadership.

After several spoke, I asked her, "Now do you know why those girls are sitting
so close to you?"

This time she nodded.

"None of the girls—or anyone else who spoke—felt the way they did based on
how much you have achieved," I said. "They talked about inner qualities that
make up who you are, how you are, and what you are. These kinds of qualities
are not measured by achievement. They come from inside of you and are part of
what makes you Joan. And they will always be a part of you, no matter what you
do or do not achieve.

"Your parents' relationship is not your responsibility," I said. "It is theirs and it
is not your job to save it for them. They have to do that themselves. And you
cannot make up for your brother, nor do you have to. You don't have to make
up for anyone or anything. You are good enough the way you are.

"Slow down," I added. "See about working fewer hours. Talk to your coach
about it. He can help. And listen to what your friends are saying to you. You are
loved, right now, just as you are. Let that in and bask in it for awhile.

"Are your parents—your father—coming to the Parents' Seminar tomorrow?"
I asked.

She had asked them to come, she said, but she wasn't sure they would.

The father did come. The mother did not. When the seminar ended, Joan entered the room, went to her father, and brought him up to meet me. He was polite, but asked no questions, and soon left.

Emotional outbursts such as this father's are usually caused by pent-up emotions, anger, and frustrations that have begun years before. They can extend way back to adolescence and even childhood, when suppressing day-to-day emotions was the only way one could deal with life.

Unfortunately, the effects of pent-up day-to-day emotions often impact other people more than the person carrying them. When someone is on the receiving end of an outburst, particularly a son or daughter, he or she ends up getting hit by a huge charge of emotion, way out of proportion to the immediate incident. An apology can be made for an outburst—most often it is not—but even if it is, sometimes it is too late. Feelings can be hurt, trusts are tested, and relationships between parent and child can be severely damaged if this kind of blowup is repeated often enough.

Angry blowups are only one consequence of a buildup of suppressed emotions. There are others. Sarcastic comments laced with anger, self-pity used to manipulate someone, humor used in a hurtful way, hostile actions, and withdrawal in order to punish another are all common ways pent-up day-to-day emotions leak or burst out on someone.

The result of any emotional outbreak can be seen and felt—children get hurt, frightened, and intimidated. Yet, there are a considerable number of parents who will not even consider taking the time to look at what they are feeling, let alone take responsibility for how their feelings might be affecting their children. Those children talk to me of their constant fear of their parents' blowups, impatience, quick temper, and hurtful judgment, which are all signs of pent-up emotions.

One of the saddest results of pent-up emotions being continually dumped on children is that, over time, children can withdraw from their own parents out of fear. The parents rarely see it. They are too emotionally suppressed to notice. The children will not talk about their fear—they are too frightened of their parent's reaction. And if a child's fear builds up too much, that child will protect himself by creating more and more distance between himself and his parent. In many families, distance between a parent and a son or daughter has existed since late childhood. When the "child" reaches his twenties, thirties, or forties, the distance only increases.

There is one important thing to remember: It is natural to sometimes have a blowup of anger or hurt, or any other emotion that may have become pent-up.

Children, especially adolescents, can do things that hurt you and make you very angry. Things can happen during the day that emotionally affect you more than you realize.

The goal here is not to become emotionally controlled and never to act inappropriately. None of us are in total control of our emotions, nor are we always aware of how we are feeling. If we think we are, we are in trouble.

The idea is to try to be as real and aware of your emotions in the present time as you can (feel your feelings while you are experiencing them instead of stuffing them down inside of you). Conscious expression will allow your emotions to flow through you rather than become pent-up. You may not always express yourself perfectly, but at least it can be with awareness and a sense of responsibility.

The more you are conscious with your expression, the greater the security you offer your children. Then, when those times come along when you reactively blow up or express yourself inappropriately, your children will know it is not your normal behavior. It does not make you frightening to them, but rather human. And most important, it will not damage their trust in you—for you will have established a track record of behavior that is more consistent and different. An apology and an explanation as to why you reacted this way can be effective and easily accepted. And you are then a responsible role model for them to look up to, one who can teach them about relationships and how to respond to their own emotions.

CHAPTER 10

Consciously
Feeling Your
Emotions

One of the first things to consider and remember when learning about your emotions, whether for the first time or at a deeper level, is that it takes courage to be honest. It is also very good for your self esteem. You are going to discover feelings that you are unaware of, and you are going to change.

There are certain activities you can start doing right away to help you become more aware, open, and expressive with your emotions. Even if you have had many years of experience expressing your feelings, you will find these suggestions very effective.

Perhaps the first place to start is by remembering this simple sentence: If you want to learn how to become more expressive with your emotions, you must begin by *consciously taking the time* to express them. Few people—parents or not—actually do this on a regular basis. You will find that the expression of your feelings is one of the most effective methods of "healing" yourself that you have available to you.

Here are two ways of working with your feelings that will help you learn to express yourself. The first involves writing. The second uses visualization.

Journaling

When working with your emotions, sometimes the best place to start is by writing them out.

No matter how aware and expressive of your emotions you currently are, journaling can be valuable to you. It can be especially helpful in learning to release day-to-day feelings, preventing them from building up inside of you.

One of the best and safest ways of learning to express your emotions is to begin writing in a journal every day, or at least every other day (if you cannot find the time, begin with once a week). When you begin, write for at least fifteen minutes a day—twenty to thirty minutes is better.

The key is consistency. Commit to continuing this process over a period of time—three months is a good time frame to begin with, though you may always want to continue journaling. You will see that the more you do it, the better and more effective it becomes.

A journal is not a diary in which you record events. Its purpose is to help you express your feelings safely, without having to worry about how someone might react. You write about the events that went on during the day or since the last time you wrote in your journal, writing specifically how you felt or how you are still feeling. Write any way you want: in phrases or complete sentences, with a series of disconnected words, whatever. Ask questions, then answer them. Or just let a stream of consciousness come out of you. The key here is to feel what you are writing.

Write Down How You Feel about These Questions in Your Journal

1. **Your Relationship with Your Children**
   How do I feel about them?
   What do I need to talk to them about?
   Am I angry at them?
   How can I love them more? What needs of theirs do I need to pay more attention to?
   How have they changed my life?
   Do I need to forgive them for something?
   What am I going to miss the most when they move out?
   How can they help me more?
   Have they hurt me in any way—and do I need to talk to them about it?

2. **Your Spouse**
   What do I need to talk to him or her about?
   How can I love him or her more?
   How do I need him or her to love me more?
   Do I need to forgive him or her for anything?
   Do I need help with anything?
   Are we spending enough time together?
   How much has my life changed because of this person?
   What are my dreams for our future?

3. **Yourself**

How can I nurture myself more?
Am I nurturing myself at all?
Do I know how to love myself?
What can my children do to help me more?
What do I need to forgive myself for?
What guilts do I need to let go of?
Do I give myself enough credit for what I am doing?
Do I judge myself too harshly?

4. **Your Friends**

How do I feel about my best friend?
How can I give more to him or her?
Do I need to talk to him or her about anything?
Are there any unresolved angers or hurts?
How much do I let this person care for me?
How often do I tell my friend how valuable he or she is to me?

5. **Your Family**

How important is my family to me? Why?
What problems do I have with my family that I need to address, but
    am afraid to?
Who do I need to forgive?
What suppressed emotions toward a family member do I need to let
    go of?
Who can I love more?
Who do I need to talk to?
What does my family do for me that I cherish?
Who do I need to thank?
How do I feel about how my mother or father treats my children?

6. **You and Your Emotions**

Which emotions scare me the most? Why?
How much love do I let myself feel—for others, for myself?
Which constricting emotions am I holding on to—anger, hurt, fear,
    despair, rage, etc.?
Which emotions do I need to feel more of—love, laughter, happi-
    ness, awe, wonder, passion?
What is blocking me from feeling certain emotions? Do I have old
    pains, angers, hurts, or other suppressed feelings inside of me?
Do I need help in learning how to heal myself?
How do I feel about needing help—about asking for help?
How much does intimacy scare me?

> Who do I share genuine intimacy with in my life?
> How much intimacy do I have with myself?

7. What It Is Like Writing in Your Journal
> What am I learning from writing?
> How has this helped me become more aware of my feelings?
> How has this helped me love myself?
> How many of my own needs have I discovered that I do not pay enough attention to?
> How rewarding is it to take time for myself?
> How has this helped me be a better parent?

These are just a few of the myriad of subjects you can explore. It does not matter so much what you write, but rather that you *feel* what you are writing. Your journal is private. No one else is to read it, unless you choose to share it. Privacy is important. It will allow you to open up to your deeper emotions more freely.

The Anger/Frustration Letter

The anger/frustration letter is a technique that, though different in intent, goes hand in hand with journaling. In other words, you can use journaling to help you explore, become aware of, and express your feelings. But if you find you are angry or frustrated, then do an anger/frustration letter on separate pieces of paper. This will let you focus specifically on letting go of either of these two emotions.

The way you write an anger/frustration letter is to write to the person you are particularly angry at or frustrated with as if you are actually writing them a real letter—but you do not mail this letter. The purpose of writing it is to give yourself a way to express and feel your emotions. This will allow you to let them go. Express everything you feel until there is no anger or frustration left—do not hold anything back.

You can also use this technique to write about a situation rather than a specific person you are frustrated or angry about. It is a very effective way to let go of your emotions.

The Steps to Writing an Anger/Frustration Letter
1. Write out your anger or frustration to the person or about the situation. Use however many pieces of paper it takes. The key is to feel what you are writing.
2. Continue writing until you reach the core or bottom of your anger

or frustration. This is the most important part of the process. If you get to the core of your feelings, you can let them go.

Most people make the mistake of feeling only part of their anger or frustration. They do not want to take the time and effort to go all the way to the bottom of their emotions. Then they wonder why their letters never work. Unfortunately, they end up fueling their emotions by only partially feeling them rather than letting them go.

3. When you are finished and there is no emotion left to feel (it could take you twenty minutes or two hours), sign your name at the end of the letter. Symbolically tell your subconscious that you are letting go of the emotion.

4. Burn each page of the letter one by one, or rip the pages into little pieces and flush them down the toilet. You are done.

The Three-Day Letter

If you are feeling a lot of anger—many pages of it—stretch your letter into a three-day process—three *consecutive* days.

1. Do the first day as described above in steps 1 through 4, but this time instead of burning it or flushing it, "hide" the letter in a private place (a drawer, a book, etc.). Hiding it is symbolic of the subconscious, of the hidden, deeper anger in you.

2. Take the letter out on the second day and read through it, feeling your anger all over again, adding whatever you need to add. Then hide the letter for one more night.

3. Repeat step 2 on the third day, but this time instead of hiding it again, burn or flush the letter. You are done.

Whenever you work with expressing and letting go of anger or frustration, it is wise to also do a "hurt" letter. Most often anger is a reaction to being hurt. If you are hurt, and keep it suppressed inside of you, any anger that you do let go of will eventually build up again—because you are still hurt.

The Hurt Letter

1. Follow steps 1 through 4 as if you are writing an anger/frustration letter, but express your hurt instead. An important difference between the two letters is that when you are writing a hurt letter, you should limit the time of duration to no more than twenty minutes (though you may do less than twenty minutes). Feeling hurt takes more out of you psychologically than feeling anger or frustration. You still want to get to the core of your hurt, but just do it in a twenty-minute framework.

2. Another difference between anger and hurt is that often hurt does not completely go away with just one emotional release. And you do

not do three-day processes with hurt like you do with anger. You may have to write two or three different *individual* letters—over several days or weeks—before it is gone. You can also write them on consecutive days if you wish, but do not save the same letter and read it each day like you do when dealing with anger—you write a *new* letter each day.

It is important to understand that sometimes after completing a hurt letter, you may feel like you are finished with your hurt—then two months later you begin feeling hurt again. This is quite normal—and this is the time to do another hurt letter. Hurt is the type of emotion that can take, depending on how deep the hurt is, a day, weeks, months, or even longer to let go.

3. It is valuable to remember that even if it takes time to let all of your hurt go, each time you do a hurt letter you are more healed and more emotionally open.

The Healing Power of Visualization

Visualization can be an incredibly easy and very effective way to feel and let go of your emotions. Most of us do it all the time whenever we are angry, frustrated, hurt, or enraged at someone or something. How many times have you been driving down the freeway or walking down the street and imagined yourself talking to someone you were very angry at or hurt by? How often have you even yelled at them right there in your car, seeing their face in your mind as if you were really talking to them? Without necessarily knowing it, you were using a very valuable technique to release your emotions. It is called visualization.

One reason why visualization works so well is that it allows you to safely express anything and everything you are feeling without the risk that the person you are expressing it to will react negatively or retaliate. And when you visualize yourself talking to someone, it feels like you are having a real conversation, which makes it easier to express yourself.

The key to effective visualization is to make it as real as you can. Sense the person you are talking to hearing everything you are saying. Express yourself in any way that will help you feel your emotions—if it makes you feel good to shout in your visualization, then shout. The idea is to use visualization to help you *feel* your feelings. And, as in the anger/frustration letter, do not stop expressing yourself until you have reached the core or bottom of your emotion—until there is nothing left to feel. Do not hold anything back. Feel deeply and completely.

You can learn to let go of any emotion using visualization, even feelings you had when you were younger. Just go back to the age you were when the incident took place and play it through in your imagination as it happened. Then replay it. This time though, *change* what happened. This time you are going to express all the feelings—anger, hurt, etc.—you were feeling at the time, the feelings you could not or did not express because the person would not let you, you were too frightened, or you thought you had no right to express.

This simple technique is remarkably effective because it takes you back to when the incident happened, allowing the "you" at that age to finally express and let go of what may have been suppressed for years. This type of visualization—working with your past—can heal the source of emotional pain and patterns that have been locked away for years. Visualization is the most effective way to release emotions from your past. Letters are more effective for current emotions.

When you are visualizing and feeling anger, hurt, or any other emotions, do not drive your car. It is dangerous. The intense focus and emotions can distract you and cause an accident. Do your visualizations only when you have uninterrupted time and privacy available to you.

Once you become more comfortable expressing your feelings in your journal, in your anger/frustration/hurt letters, and by using visualization, you can begin expressing some of these feelings directly to your family and friends. Start with emotions that are easier to express, working toward the more difficult ones.

A good way to start is to first express yourself in writing or in visualization. This will allow you to let go of some of the emotional charge you are carrying around inside of you. It can make it a lot easier to then express yourself to the actual person.

What if someone might be hurt by what you are going to say? As long as you are expressing yourself out of respect for yourself and the truth—and *without intent* to consciously hurt or blame that person—you owe your family and friends the truth. Sometimes the person may be hurt anyway, by the very nature of what you need to tell him or her. If your true intent is to improve the relationship, to clear something up because you care enough about them, your relationship can only benefit by your honesty. If you do not express how you feel, you will always have something unresolved between you and the other person, but that person will never know what it is.

This works two ways, of course. The other person also needs to be able to talk to you about his or her own feelings—and your impact on them. Two-way, open conversation is how intimate and trusting relationships are developed. They take practice and patience, and there is always a risk of being hurt, but the closeness and love can bring unending joy and happiness.

There is one truism about relationships: If you want love in your life, you have to be vulnerable enough to let someone love you. This also means you or the other person can be hurt, even in the best of relationships. Hurt, anger, fear, happiness, joy, and any other emotion are all parts of relationships. Without these different emotions you cannot have a relationship with any real meaning or depth.

You are not perfect, nor are the people you love and care about. Yet if you are willing to be honest and open in how you express yourself, you can learn to mitigate the hurt and build a solid, trusting, intimate relationship.

Perhaps one way to look at this is that hurting people and damaging people are very different from each other. Hurting someone pertains to doing or saying something that causes that person to feel the specific emotion of hurt. When you damage someone you may cause that person to feel one or several emotions—hurt, anger, shame, humilation, fear, despair—and you *always* take away from their sense of worth, value, and dignity. Talking to someone—with responsibility and the intent to resolve a situation—may hurt that person, but it will not damage him or her.

If you ask the people you care about if they would rather you hide the truth from them because you are afraid they might be hurt, what do you think they would say? How many would want to know how you feel, even at the risk of being hurt?

As a way to remind yourself of your responsibility—before you have your conversation with the person you need to talk with—you might ask yourself, "What is my intent in this conversation?"

Learning to express your feelings does take courage. You have to feel your own feelings and cope with another's reaction. It also takes practice. Though you may never feel totally comfortable expressing certain emotions, if you are willing to begin learning to share your feelings more openly, it will eventually become a natural part of your communication.

Journaling, anger/frustration/hurt letters, and visualization are very effective techniques for both discovering and expressing your feelings. They can help prevent you from becoming pent-up with day-to-day emotions, as well as open the doors for you to recognize, feel, and release other emotions you may have been suppressing for years. As you become more familiar and open with your feelings, you can build a deeper emotional awareness and a more meaningful sense of intimacy within yourself and your family.

If you discover that you have past pains or traumatic situations that you have either not dealt with or do not know how to deal with, there are many things you can do to help heal yourself.
❒ Try using the techniques suggested in this book. They are very effective and have been used by thousands of people with success.
❒ You can always seek professional help.

❐ Read books and articles (your local bookstore and library have a wealth of information ready to explore) to learn more about the areas you want to heal.

❐ Attend seminars.

❐ Meditation/visualization is an invaluable tool in healing, and there are a variety of audio tapes available that can prove most helpful in dealing with specific emotional areas.

❐ Do not forget your spouse, family members, and friends. They might know some excellent resources.

❐ The more you can learn about what you want to heal and change, the easier it will be to do it.

Part of the incentive for taking charge of your emotions is to try to heal any constricting emotions and patterns of behavior that will negatively affect your children. Having children involved in competitive athletics, where there is already a good deal of emotional pressure, is an even greater motivation not to add any more to their "emotional plate."

At the same time, no one is perfect. Nor will anyone always do or say the right thing. You may not even recognize a pattern that is obvious to everyone else. Yet if you are willing to put forth the effort and time in looking at yourself honestly and openly, you can usually discover the origins of your patterns.

If you are willing to go even further, to learn to heal whatever patterns you find, you can open a door to an entirely different experience in life. You can emerge stronger and more capable of feeling fulfillment, love, happiness, and joy. And the way you relate to others, especially your children, can change, allowing for more understanding, compassion, and support.

As a final note, keep in mind that being emotionally open and expressive does not guarantee that your children will open up to you. But it does, at the very least, guarantee opportunities for them to do so. Being emotionally closed and unexpressive guarantees *no* opportunities.

CHAPTER 11

Unresolved Issues with Your Parents

Because your most vulnerable and impressionable years were spent with your parents, it is impossible not to have been heavily influenced by everything they said and did. These influences will manifest in how you currently feel about yourself, and how you relate to others—children, spouses, in-laws, friends, authority figures, and business associates.

The most significant influence parents have on their children will always be emotional. And none of us can escape the fact that if we still carry unresolved emotional issues with our parents, we will pass them down to our own children.

For example, if your parents were expressive and emotionally open, you will have been taught by example to be open. If they were emotionally closed, you will follow their lead and become closed yourself. They essentially taught you—by example—to suppress your emotions.

For some, our parents' influence has been more positive and expanding. For others, it has been more constrictive and damaging. For the greatest number, it is a combination of both expanding and constricting influences.

The positive influences typically will be about loving, moral standards, humor, friendship, nurturing, and other similar issues. The constricting influences are usually tied up with unresolved issues, such as, anger, hurt, betrayal, abandonment, shame, and physical/emotional abuse.

Constricting influences—too many of which can cause dysfunction—result from parents who never healed their own angers, hurts, or shame. They passed on their constrictions—and dysfunctions—to their children through their behavior: controlling, comparing, demanding, etc.

Whatever your parents' influence may have been, you absorbed it into your subconscious as you grew up. It became a part of who you are, played out through your actions, reactions, thoughts, and feelings. Unless you have *consciously* changed that influence, no matter what your age, it is still a part of you.

Being influenced by your parents is inescapable. But it is only a problem when that influence is based upon unresolved issues that are still causing constrictions or dysfunction in your life. Then it becomes at the very least limiting, and more often damaging to you and to those around you.

Recognizing Unresolved Issues

Unresolved issues, in the context of our relationship with our parents, stem from unexpressed/suppressed emotional issues that developed as we grew through childhood and adolescence. Anything that we have not yet resolved from those growing-up years will be an issue now in our life. Such issues include conflicts in love relationships, fear of expressing certain emotions, fear of being wrong, a need for control, and others.

Perhaps the most difficult problem we face in recognizing unresolved issues is that most of us are not familiar with how deeply our emotions affect us. We usually *assume* how angry or hurt or afraid we might be, but how often do we really take the time to actually let ourselves feel the emotion? We can be aware of an emotion, feeling it rise up inside of us; but unless we feel that emotion *deeply,* for however long it takes for it to dissipate, we cannot genuinely understand how much it is affecting us.

Another common assumption is that emotions just go away in time, all by themselves. Time heals all, or something like that. While there may be some diminishing of our emotions, like hurt, over a period of time, emotions do not just go away all by themselves.

This is evidenced by reactions we continually repeat—often for years—to the same emotional stimuli, such as a fear of someone becoming angry at us. How often do we stop and ask ourselves why are we so afraid of angering someone? What is the source of this fear? Do we just continue to react in fear without thinking about it?

If we do look at such behavior, we will more than likely discover that it began long ago, in our childhood or adolescence. Time may have dimmed our memory of it, but our emotional reaction can be as strong today as it was many years ago when it began. We have an emotional memory that exists in our consciousness—not in our intellect. Unresolved/suppressed emotions cannot be explained away or ignored. Suppressing our feelings, even to the point of not consciously feeling them anymore, will not make them go away. It just pushes them deeper into our subconscious.

Does that mean we need to deal with every suppressed emotion we ever experienced with our parents in order to clear up unresolved issues? Certainly not. That could take us the rest of our lives. We do need to deal with the more important ones, though, the ones that have the most constricting effects upon our lives.

Where does one look for these emotions? They are usually found in repeated patterns of behavior—charged reactive behavior, always having to be right, avoiding dealing with certain emotions, the need for control, withdrawing when angry, never feeling good enough, perfectionism.

Whatever our patterns happen to be, we are the only ones who can change them. Though this might seem rather obvious, I have met a significant number of parents of young athletes who have been relating to their children through a specific pattern of behavior for years, often without even seeing it:

During a Parent's Seminar, a father raised his hand and started to speak then stopped, shook his head, paused, and began again.

"There is something I do with my son that I know I should stop doing, but I can't seem to stop," he said, shaking his head. "I have this need to continually give my son advice—even when he does not want that advice. I mean he flat out tells me to stop, that he already has a coach. He doesn't need another one.

"My son is a really good athlete. "There are just these things that I always see—that I think will help him if he only knew about them—and I want to tell him."

He shrugged his shoulders, shook his head, and laughed. "I know it sounds ridiculous," he said.

"It is not at all ridiculous," I said. "You care a great deal for your son. In your heart you want to help him. The question is: Why do you continue to do something he does not want you to do—which is not helpful? Do you have any idea why you have this need to coach your son? Have you ever really thought about it, and tried to find the source?"

He considered the question for a while, and then shook his head. "I am aware of the need, particularly as my son is growing older and is relying more on his coach rather than me, but I have no idea where it comes from—or even where to begin to look," he said.

"Do you mind if I ask you some questions—to help you look?"

"No. Please do. I would like some help in understanding it," he answered.

"Okay. Good," I said. Then I began. "Let me ask you this. Are you afraid the coach might fail in some way—that he might miss something—and that is why you feel the need to always give advice—to make sure your son won't fail?"

He thought about that for awhile. And then, "As silly as it sounds," he replied, "I *am* afraid the coach might miss something. I feel like I need to be kind of a backup coach. You know, just in case."

"When you were younger, how was it between you and your father?" I asked him.

He replied with a slow shake of his head. "He was always correcting and criti-
cizing me. If I were to sum it up in one sentence: Whatever I did was never good
enough for my father. And you know, it still isn't to this day." There was such a
change in his energy and tone of voice when he spoke; his mouth seemed to
harden, lips pressed tightly together.

"What did it do to you—to feel like you could never be good enough for your
father?" I asked.

"I felt like he ground me into the dirt," he answered. "I tried everything to
please him. I was a great student, a responsible kid. I didn't lie. But nothing I did
was ever quite good enough for him. It was like, in his eyes, there was always
something wrong with me."

"You know, the way you were raised is a familiar story for a great number of
people," I began. "Your father made you feel like something was wrong with
you by repeatedly disapproving of you—no matter what you did. He eventually
convinced you that you were not good enough, not just as a student or a son,
but as a person—as a human being. Whatever was lacking in his life, he took out
on you. He did this by making you the reflection of his own lack, his own sense
of not being good enough.

"Feeling 'not good enough' or 'flawed' is the definition of shame," I continued. "Shame is passed down—unless healed—from generation to generation.
He passed his shame down to you. It caused a deep and terrible pain of separation from your father, one that made you feel flawed and unlovable. And that
part of you—the shamed boy and teenager—still exists to this day inside of you,
just below the surface, in your subconscious. For example, how did you feel
when I asked you about your father?"

"Just thinking about my childhood brings up all those feelings all over again,"
he answered. "Is this at the root of my need to coach my son?"

"Let me ask you," I answered. "How would you feel if your son failed as an
athlete—that he somehow never reached his potential?"

"Terrible," he said. "I would wonder what I could have done to prevent it."

"Now do you know why you need to coach him?" I asked. "The shame buried
inside of you, yet always present—just below the surface—is manifesting as a
fear that somehow you will not be good enough as a father—just like you were
not good enough as a son.

"Shame," I continued, "makes us feel like we need to always do something
extra to make up for our feeling of not being good enough. One of the things
you do extra is to obsessively coach your son—even when he doesn't need or
want it. This way you can prove you are a good enough father by trying to make
sure your son succeeds. The problem here is that if he should fail, you will blame
yourself—since you have made yourself responsible for his success—bringing the
shame that you carry inside of you right to the surface, causing you to relive the
pain of your father's criticisms all over again.

He looked stunned, as if someone had punched him.

"I just realized how true that is," he said, shaking his head. "I always feel like if my son fails in any way, it's my fault—that in some way I have failed him."

"As you sit there, more aware at this point," I said, "let me ask you. How do you think your son might feel being constantly coached by you, being forced to shoulder your need to succeed—whether he likes it or not?"

He did not answer right away. "I've got to be putting a lot of pressure on him," he finally said. "And I know he is angry at me."

"One more question," I said. "What message are you giving your son when you are constantly telling him what he could or should do to improve himself?"

There was another pause while he considered the question. "Though it looks a little different," he began, "by constantly giving him advice on how to be better, I'm telling him he isn't good enough the way he is. I can't believe it! I'm acting just like my father."

"Why don't you sit down and talk to your son?" I told him. "Explain to him what you have become aware of and how you realize it must affect him. Apologize to him. He will hear you—he loves you. And then tell him about your father, how you were raised, how it has affected your way of seeing yourself and your role as a father—that his success is your responsibility not his. Give your son a chance to understand you, and give yourself a chance to understand your son's needs."

"I think that is a good idea," he said.

"Your father never took the time to do that for you," I said. "But you will do this for your son. And that is the difference between you and your father."

We ended the conversation speaking about different books he might read to help him learn about healing shame. I thanked him for his honesty and his vulnerability.

I then asked how many other parents—mothers and fathers—in the room, all of whom had been following our conversation for the last twenty minutes, could relate to his situation. Nearly half of them raised their hands. Several had tears in their eyes.

All of us have some constricting patterns. We develop them in our childhood and teen years. It is a normal and unavoidable part of growing up.

The father I just spoke of and all the other fathers and mothers who are similar to him in the way they act out their emotional patterns toward their children are not "screwed up, bad parents." Rather, they are simply carrying constricting, unresolved feelings of hurt, shame, anger, and other emotions that have distorted their sense of worth. Any issue of self-worth will always lead to constricting behavioral patterns.

The good news is that any pattern of behavior can be changed, or at the very least mitigated, if you are willing to heal your unresolved emotions. Once healed, you can be emotionally free to recognize your inherent worth and value—without the distortion of shame and other such damaging emotions. You can then develop new patterns of behavior that will positively change your relationship with those you love, particularly your children.

The first place to look for your patterns and unresolved emotions is in your own primary family. How were you raised? What were you told, and how were you treated? How did it influence you and make you feel? Were father and mother emotionally there for you? How did your parents relate to each other?

To find answers to these questions, you need to look honestly and closely at your relationship with your parents during your childhood and adolescent years.

Your Parents' Issues Were Passed Down to You

Whatever emotional issues your parents had when you were growing up were passed down to you. How they have manifested in you is for you to recognize and change.

It is easy to look at how your parents act and even at how they affect you, yet it is not so easy to see them in the same light as other people—without the filter of "Mom and Dad" in front of your eyes. You can be blinded by childhood loyalties and a sense of obligation and duty. And whatever fears, guilt, anger, and other such constricting emotions you might have will affect your perception. All these things added together can muddy the water when you are trying to see the truth about your parents' behavior.

The simple truth is that *everyone*—your parents included—has unresolved issues and constricting patterns of behavior until they consciously heal and change them. If you can recognize the particular issues your parents had when you were growing up, it will help you discover your own. In other words, how they behaved toward you and each other when you were growing up is intricately linked to how you behave. Whatever emotional issues your current pattern represents—issues of trust, need to be perfect, need to be right, need to control, difficulty expressing feelings—will be linked in some way to your relationship with your parents.

While most people are certainly aware of their parents' behavior, how many consciously take the time to look deeper to understand the profound connection between their parents' behavior and their own? How many are not even remotely aware of their own patterns and are unwittingly passing them down to their children, just as their parents did to them?

It takes both courage and love to look honestly at how your parents treated you when you were growing up. Courage is needed because you might see things that will stir up a lot of deeper emotions. If that is so, then good. It is possible to heal these emotions once you can get to them. And love is needed so you will not judge your parents—or yourself—in your quest for discovery, healing, and change.

Emotional Patterns

As it takes courage to look with honesty at your parents' behavior, it also takes courage to look at yourself, to open doors to certain feelings that you have closed long ago—usually because of pain.

It is challenging to explore your hidden feelings and to look at your deeper motivations. Yet to love your children, to be able to understand them with wisdom and insight, to not pass on to them your feelings of shame and other constricting emotions, you need to take responsibility for your patterns and do your best to change them.

While patterns of behavior are usually based upon your relationship with your parents, some incidents that happen outside your parents' influence can also cause behavioral patterns as you are growing up. These are typically found with siblings, relatives, childhood and adolescent friends, teachers, coaches, grandparents, and isolated incidents. While the focus in this particular section is on how your parents' behavior affected you, if there happens to be a pattern linked to something or someone outside your family, it is wise to deal with it, in addition to any issues you see with your parents. The constricting emotions causing these other patterns need to be treated in the same manner as any unresolved emotional issues.

CHAPTER 12

Finding Your
Emotional
Patterns

The following steps are designed to help you find your particular behavioral patterns. Take your time. Explore your feelings, thoughts, and memories. Talk with your spouse or a friend if you need insight. Write out your feelings. Come back and look again. As you discover one thing, it will lead to another.

The purpose here is to explore, to discover, in order to be able to heal, change, and grow.

1. Everyone Has Emotional Patterns

The first step is to realize that everyone has emotional patterns of behavior. They are formed during your childhood and adolescent years and have a great deal to do with your relationship with your mother and father. Your patterns are also strongly influenced by birth order (see Question 3 in Chapter 13, "The Seven Questions Parents Ask Most"), and sometimes by siblings, friends, or other authority figures—like coaches.

It is also helpful to keep in mind that most patterns of behavior based on constricted emotions are developed to protect you in one way or another from the pain of being separated from love. So much of the time when people feel anger and hurt and despair, it is because they are not being loved the way they want to be loved.

Typical examples of emotional patterns can be readily seen. There is the need to control, the fear of commitment, perfectionism, the need to constantly achieve, avoidance of success, fear of betrayal and abandonment, the need to rescue, being the clown to gain attention, and so on.

2. Be Aware of Your Feelings

Look at how you act when you feel fear, anger, hurt, embarrassment, sadness, love, happiness, guilt, shame, and other emotions. Do you become anxious, aggressive, withdrawn, depressed, defensive, hostile, controlling? Do you want to talk about your feelings—or withdraw and avoid dealing with them all together? Do you want to go do something to take your mind off of things? Do you want to eat, smoke, take a drug, drink, or work out to numb yourself?

If you are willing to be honest, you will begin to see patterns. Most are not hidden. If you have any doubts about what you see, ask those closest to you what they see. They are aware of how you act.

3. Chart Your Emotional History

Look back to see how many years you have acted in a specific way in specific situations or relationships. How long, in other words, have you had this pattern of behavior? Does it go back to your twenties, your teens, your childhood?

An excellent way of finding out is to get a sense of how this pattern feels. There is always a feeling or a series of feelings associated with a pattern: First I feel angry, then I feel hurt, then afraid, etc. To find these feelings, close your eyes and replay the last time you recall displaying your current pattern.

What are you feeling when you are acting out your pattern? You may have to do this several times to accurately recognize what you are feeling. The feelings you are most uncomfortable or familiar with are usually the source of your pattern.

Once you recognize the feelings, take yourself back five years earlier in your life and try to find these same feelings there. If you do find it, look at when you felt it. What happened that caused the feeling? Look for your pattern. You will find it. Now go back another five years and repeat the same process. Continue exploring further and further into your past at five-year intervals to get a sense of when the pattern started (you can shorten the intervals if you get below twelve years of age). This will give you clues as to its origins.

4. Discover the Origins of Your Emotional Patterns

Look to see if your pattern is connected to your relationship with your father or mother (or sister, brother, grandparent, friend, coach, teacher, etc.). Can you connect this pattern with a specific incident, or repeated incidences, or did you see something happen? If you can, this will give you an understanding of what happened and why you began the pattern. It is not always easy to discover the origins of your patterns, and it may take some time and looking to find the truth, but you can do it if you have the desire.

Common sources of pain from which patterns of behavior are developed to protect you from that pain are issues of abandonment, control, betrayal, humiliation, loss, rejection, physical and/or emotional abuse, and the granddaddy of them all—shame. Look to see which of these pains you may have experienced—once or repeatedly—when you were younger. You may have experienced all of them. Which pain, or pains, stands out?

One clue in looking is to see what scares you the most in your life today. Another is to look at which of these pains you find yourself repeatedly experiencing—in the same relationship or in all relationships. And a third clue is to ask yourself which pain you would do nearly anything to avoid.

As you sift through your feelings about your relationship with your parents, exploring your childhood and adolescent experiences, you can discover much about your emotional patterns of behavior—then and now.

How did you deal with fear, stress, hurt, and pain then? How do you deal with those same feelings now? Many of your survival and security issues are going to show up as patterns of behavior that began long ago from a need to get your parents' love—and to protect you from the pain of losing it.

The idea is to explore the relationship with your parents to see if there are any old patterns of behavior still current in your life now. Maybe, in one way or another, you have successfully changed them. But the chances are very likely that they are, perhaps to a large degree, still operating. If so, how are these patterns now affecting your relationship with your spouse and children?

There is a very important thing to always remember when doing this work. If you find in looking at your behavior that you feel guilty for things you have said or done, you can always learn to forgive yourself. In fact, one of the biggest blocks to personal growth is our fear that we are going to find out things about ourselves that make us feel shameful. Self-forgiveness—not self-blame—is always the appropriate solution. If you do not know how to forgive yourself, there are many books and counselors available to help you learn.

Your relationships with your mother and father are complex, and they affect you on unseen levels. The very development of your thinking and feeling processes throughout your child/adolescent years was indelibly affected by your parents. Fully understanding the far-reaching effects of their impact upon you can take, for many, years to understand.

When exploring your relationship with your parents, it is wise to use all resources available. It is often very difficult to accurately see and understand your own family patterns because you are so close to them.

Going through the process of recognizing and changing your emotional patterns will give you a depth of understanding about many of your primary emotional needs. You will feel and see things that no book or lecture could ever reveal to you.

Understanding your childhood fears, pains, and emotional needs will give you an immense advantage in raising your children. You will have greater empathy and insight into their needs, and therefore know how to make them emotionally more secure. As you, in essence, add to the development of your own Whole Self—through the process of healing and letting go of your patterns—you will automatically gain a depth of understanding in knowing how to support and encourage the evolution of your children's Whole Selves.

The Value of Asking for Help

As to the process of discovering my own patterns, particularly in regard to my relationships with my parents, I found there was great value in asking for help. When I first began my inner journey of exploration, I was reluctant to ask anyone for help. I believed that just by asking I was admitting something was wrong with me—and my parents. I also believed I should be able to figure things out for myself. After all, it was my life, my family.

In time, I realized that I felt embarrassed that I was having problems with my mother and father. I did not want to admit that. And on a deeper level, I was terribly afraid I might find something inside of me that was really screwed up.

As it turned out, throughout my journey I have indeed seen things I did not like—did not want to admit to. I have felt shame and great fear, and have seen my blame and righteousness toward my parents. But through it all, I have also discovered a deeper sense of love and compassion for my parents than I could ever have imagined possible. I have learned how to heal and change—and that I am not "screwed up." I have much healthier and more fulfilling relationships with everyone in my life than ever before, especially the one with my wife, Barbara.

None of this could have happened if I had not asked for someone's help and guidance along the way.

The first person I asked for help from was based on a friend's recommendation. After that experience, which was very beneficial, I explored other avenues of help. All have offered significant value.

Who do you ask for help? It is someone who you believe can help you. It may be someone a friend has found to be valuable. You may even work with several people until you find the right one. When you are sincerely looking for help, it seems to have its own way of finding you.

Beyond Your Parents

Though your relationship with your parents is generally at the source of your major pattern of behavior, other circumstances also produce patterns of behavior. You may have experienced a devastating failure in athletics or school or some other arena that was very important to you. On a more tragic level, rape, molestation, the unexpected death of a parent or a friend, or any other kind of traumatic event can easily cause a life-changing reaction.

There are many young athletes—and parents—who have been repeatedly humiliated by coaches, or sometimes even by other athletes, to the point where one day they emotionally break. Perhaps they make a decision about themselves that they are worthless and unlovable, or they may simply lose their confidence. This feeling or decision, unless changed, can influence them for the rest of their lives. Unfortunately, I know many who have never recovered from experiences like this. They are capable of healing, but most have decided to keep their pain buried.

Though these kinds of situations are not linked to your parents, they can just as easily create unresolved emotional issues and patterns of behavior:

During a Parent's Seminar, a mother raised her hand. We had been talking about competition and how upset many young athletes become when they lose.

"I may be the only one in here who feels this way, but I have to say this," she began. "I cannot understand the value of a highly competitive, time-consuming sport—or why my daughter is so committed to it. I'm baffled by it."

She hesitated and looked around at the other parents. No one said anything, so she continued.

"My daughter gives her time, heart, body, and soul to her sport," she said. "And for what? She is always physically tired, has no time for herself, or for many of her school activities."

"It is a situation many young athletes face," I said.

"The greatest difficulty I have with the whole thing," she added, "is in watching her feel such disappointment and pain whenever she fails in a competition. She really gets hurt over some of her losses. I always feel so hurt when she gets hurt. I don't know what to do to help her."

She stopped and shook her head, clearly bothered by just the thought of her daughter feeling hurt.

"Why would she want to put herself in a position to get hurt like that?" she asked. "I just don't understand why she stays with it—why anyone stays with it. I've tried to talk her out of competing several times, but she won't listen to me."

There was something in the way the mother spoke about competition that made me curious as to why she seemed so one-sided about the issue, so unable to grasp her daughter's sense of commitment for her sport. It was as if she herself was the one who was uncomfortable with competitive sports, that this was not about her daughter, but rather about her in some way. I decided to take a shot at what I was beginning to sense was really going on.

"Were you ever involved in competitive sports when you were younger?" I asked.

She hesitated for a moment and then said, "Yes, but that was a long time ago." She added quickly, "And it was just for fun."

I looked at her, saying nothing.

"How long ago?" I asked.

"Seventh, eighth, and ninth grades," she answered.

"What was your sport?"

"Swimming."

"Just like your daughter," I said. "What a coincidence. Did you ever compete seriously—not just for fun?"

"Oh, maybe when I first started, I guess," she said. "But I wasn't very good."

"When did you decide it was 'just for fun'?" I asked.

"I don't know—sometime in there."

Her answers were suddenly coming very quickly—too quickly. I said nothing for a while, then, "Let me ask it in a different way. Did something happen to you when you were swimming?"

She seemed stunned by the question. Her hands, sitting on her lap, had begun wringing each other.

"What happened?" I asked gently.

She suddenly began to tear up, and as she was quickly wiping her eyes, she said, "I'm sorry . . . I'm sorry for becoming so emotional."

"It's alright. You don't have to apologize for feeling your emotions," I told her.

She shook her head. Though she tried, she could not stop the tears—and now they were increasing. "I don't understand this. All these feelings are coming up—from when I first began swimming," she said. "I had forgotten them."

"What happened?"

"I wanted to be part of the team—I thought I would make new friends," she began. "Everything started out so well—it was fun. I even had the hope that I might be a good swimmer one day."

She stopped and shook her head again, wiping her tears. "I'm taking up too much time—I'm sorry. I'll stop now."

"No. You are not," I said. "Please go on."

She hesitated, looking around. Several parents encouraged her to continue.

"Well," she continued, "about halfway through the season a clique of four or five girls had formed. They were the most popular and the leaders. They also were the meanest. I thought I was doing pretty well in my training and during the meets, but I knew I could improve. For some reason—even today I don't understand why—they began putting me down for little things, about my training, my results—about me personally. I tried to ignore it, but it hurt . . . so badly."

She was swallowing and blinking rapidly while she spoke.

"By the end of the season I had become their favorite target, or so it felt," she continued. "They now said things to humiliate me in public, during our meets, during practice. It was constant. It now became about how bad a swimmer I was—what a loser I was."

She suddenly caught her breath, more an involuntary sob, then tried to stop herself from crying, putting a shaking hand across her eyes, apologizing again for being so emotional. "I tried harder," she continued, "to show them I was a good swimmer, thinking that would stop them. But I swam worse and worse . . . until I was a failure."

She stopped, wrung her hands, shook her head, and said, "I didn't realize I still felt so much. I can't believe it—it was years ago, when I was a teenager, yet just thinking about those girls makes me cringe and hurt all over again."

She sat quietly for a moment, and then said, "I almost quit the team after that year, but I didn't want to give them that satisfaction, like they had won. And now as I think about it, that was when I decided I would never try my hardest again. I would continue swimming, but it would be 'just for fun.' I was not going to give them the opportunity to hurt me."

The room was silent, as it had been for close to thirty minutes. None of the other fifty or so parents had raised their hands, gone to the bathroom, or even spoken to each other.

"It is clear and understandable why you see little value in competitive sports," I began. "You were shamed, judged, and humiliated repeatedly. You became the brunt of a group of vicious teenage girls' idea of twisted fun. The hurt and pain, as you can see, is still with you today."

"I'm shocked by how much is there," she said, "I can't even remember the last time I thought about those girls."

"Emotions exist outside of time, held in your subconscious," I said. "Time has little effect upon them if they are major woundings, except in terms of our conscious memory. As you have demonstrated, one can forget some emotions. Usually it is a way of suppressing the pain associated with the incidents. It is a way of protecting ourselves, particularly when we are younger. Perhaps the most important question for you is: Do you now know why you feel so much pain when your daughter feels pain, and why you cannot see the value of competitive sports?"

She looked down and began wringing her hands again. "I'm not sure," she said. "I just think it's too much pain for her to have to face at such a young age."

"Maybe, every time she feels pain—because she is a swimmer just like you were and at the same age—you cannot help but identify with her in such a way that it taps right into your own long-suppressed pain. In other words, when you see her, you see yourself—defenseless and unable to stop the pain. If she would just stop swimming, you would not have to deal with all this pain and discomfort—hers and your own."

She looked at me, sitting very still, her hands unmoving on her lap. "You're saying that what I have been feeling—the hurt and pain—over my daughter's pain has really been my own pain, but I haven't been aware of it?" she asked.

"Not entirely," I said. "You do feel pain for your daughter when she hurts—you love her and feel for her. But you also feel your own pain that lies just below the surface, except when a trigger of some kind—in this case your daughter's pain—brings it up. The problem this presents is that you cannot separate the two sources of pain. They merge and hit you at the same time, as one big mass of pain, which makes it much more severe and much more difficult to have to feel."

She began slowly nodding. "I understand . . . now," she said. "And it makes sense when I think about it. But now I feel bad about all the things I said to my daughter that had much more to do with me than her."

"I bet your daughter will understand if you give her the opportunity," I said. "Why don't you tell her that you have become aware of something and you want to talk to her about it? Tell her about your experience as a young swimmer, what happened to you and how it has affected you. And tell her it is not her fault, nor has she been the cause of any problem. Tell her that, in fact, now that you have seen this pain, you can finally take steps to heal it and let it go. And then tell her how much you love her."

She smiled, nodding again. "I think I can do that," she said.

A father then spoke up. "When you were talking, I was thinking—and feeling. I still have so many feelings just like you from those years. It really surprised me. I know I have been saying things to my daughter because of what happened to me, without really being aware of why I felt so strongly about some things."

A number of parents thanked her, saying how valuable our conversation had been, that they too without always knowing it were often relating to their kids through their own past pains, fears, and hurts.

The room was very quiet for a minute or two. Then another father raised his hand. "I have learned so much listening to you," he said, turning to her. "I realize that it is impossible not to communicate whatever I am feeling—or have inside of me but don't know I'm feeling—to my son. One way or another I cannot hide it from him. I never saw until today how careful and aware I need to be for my son. It's a huge responsibility."

Whether an emotional issue is with your parents or from another source, any issue can be "forgotten" or minimized in your memory over time. Your own defense systems that you developed in childhood and adolescence will automatically suppress pain to protect you from feeling it.

You *need* to distance yourself from deep pain sometimes, because you simply cannot face it at the time, particularly when you are younger. It is too big, too hurtful, too overwhelming. While this automatic reaction of emotionally shutting yourself down may initially "get you through" the pain, the longer that pain is trapped inside of you without your taking steps to heal it, the more deeply suppressed it becomes. Often, after a period of time, you are not even aware you are suppressing it—because you have so numbed yourself to its effects.

As long as you are always, on some level, protecting yourself from feeling that pain, you will never let yourself feel the full range and depth of your other emotions. To do that, you would have to be willing to feel everything, including the pain.

There is a further cost of suppressing feelings. If at some point you do not take the time to deal with your emotions, they will become a part of you, finding their way into your beliefs and attitudes, influencing how you think and make decisions. And, in one way or another, whatever your suppressed emotions may be—anger, hurt, fear—they will be communicated to your children.

In the example of the mother of the swimmer, she had been unable to fully support her daughter's participation in sports. How did that affect the daughter? Could she ever really talk to her mother about her experiences in sports? Could she ever fully share her hurt and disappointment over her losses? How alone did that make her feel? And how much pain or disappointment would the daughter hide from her mother in order to avoid upsetting her? How did the mother's continual questioning of her daughter's motivation to be an athlete affect how she felt about herself?

As a parent, a major part of your role is helping your children as best you can to grow up in a loving, caring, and understanding atmosphere. It will not be a perfect one, but it does not have to be one crisscrossed with unresolved emotional issues that you are still carrying. The more you are willing to question, reflect, and continually be curious about why you act and feel the way you do, the more you can learn, heal, and grow emotionally. As you are willing to deal with your pains and hurts—past and present—you will become far more capable of creating an ever-expanding, loving, and understanding home for your children to grow up in.

If you have experienced an incident of some kind, or have been treated in such a way that has caused you to carry old fears or hurts or angers inside of you, it is worth exploring to see if you need to do further healing. This applies whether it looms large in your mind or seems distant in your past.

Questions and Answers

CHAPTER 13

The Seven Questions
Parents Ask Most

*N*o *matter where they may live,* parents ask many of the same questions. The type of sport in which their children participate has little to do with the shared issues they all face. At the same time, there is not necessarily a pat, simple answer to each question.

When you consider all the variables that come into play in a question asked by a parent—emotions, other siblings, time constraints, family conflicts, pressures in school and sports, friendships, divorces, and marriages, to name a few—the same question could be answered differently for each parent. In fact, during one seminar I actually did answer the same question three different ways. Three mothers were facing the same problem with their daughters, but each was a very different situation. Culture, parental attitudes, ages of the girls, and the different levels of communication existing between parent and daughter meant that each parent required a different approach.

What I always attempt to do when responding to parents is to offer answers and observations based upon my experiences in my own life and from working with thousands of children, teens, young adults, and parents. I also always suggest that parents take my answer, or whatever part that fits for them, and add it to what they already know. And I do my best to answer questions in a way that is directed to that particular parent.

In this book, because it is not possible to talk to you personally to find out your particular needs, the answers offered are ones I hope you can personalize. They are meant, as is the entire book, to help you begin an inward process of reflection, discovery, understanding, and change in whatever ways are most appropriate for you—to help you be more able to answer the needs of your children.

The questions offered here are the ones most frequently asked. Though there are only seven of them, the answers, as you will see, cover a lot of territory.

Question 1—"How should I act and what can I say to my children when they fail in a competition and feel devastated?"

On the surface, there is a seemingly simple answer for this question: Always be supportive, loving, and understanding. Say what you think will work best at the time, taking into consideration each particular situation and the emotional condition of your child. Be patient. Sometimes you just need to be with them, letting them work out their feelings. And perhaps most important, always let them know you are there for them. Your consistency—with your attention, interest, and care—speaks louder than any words.

Though this answer may seem simple, it is one of the most frequently asked questions—because "simple" does not always mean easy to do. It takes a lot of understanding, experience, patience, and wisdom to be able to consistently follow through with all of the things suggested. And the key to it all lies not in what you do, but rather in the strength of your emotional connection with your children.

Even if you have the emotional connection, or are building it, there are still reasons why it may be difficult to respond the way you would prefer. Sometimes your children do not want to talk to you—you are their parent, you could not possibly understand. Many young athletes want to talk to their coaches first, not you, if they want to talk at all. And there are times when your children are simply too overwhelmed with emotion. They withdraw. You do not know how to reach them.

There are many reasons why it can be difficult to know how to act or what to say. The point is that there can be different circumstances prevailing upon you and your children that make it difficult for you to always know how to respond to their needs. Perhaps the best place to start is by looking at your core responsibility in a situation where your children experience a devastating, disappointing, or painful failure.

As a parent, your responsibility is to love and support your children as best you can—you know this part. Remember that you are not superman or superwoman. You can and will make mistakes.

Recognizing this, the next step is figuring out what to say and how to act around young athletes who are hurt, angry, or disappointed after a painful loss in a competition.

One approach is to always start by making it safe for them to feel whatever emotions they are feeling—anger, hurt, pain, fear, despair—so they can let them go and move on. At the same time, it is just as important to be there for them, to understand and empathize, so they do not feel alone. This is not the time to let them know how disappointed you are in them (if you are), or to make them "wrong" for their failure, no matter how badly they did or how many things they could have or should have done differently. It is quite amazing how many parents seem to feel the need to remind their children of their failures just after they have had one, as if somehow that is going to help them.

After children have had a chance to react to their loss, which for teens or adolescents may include going off somewhere to be alone or talking to their coach, then you can say what you feel is appropriate. There are many things you could say, but what you ultimately decide to say depends upon how athletically capable your children are, how bad the loss was, the circumstances of the loss, how important the competition was, how the loss affected the team, how high the expectations were for a good performance, and any other considerations that need to be taken into account.

Sometimes a good approach when wondering what to say is to ask questions, such as: "Are you okay?" "Do you want to talk about it?" "Is there anything I can do?" This way you are leaving it up to your children to guide you as to what they need. If you happen to have very young children, five to ten years of age, then you may need to help them with their feelings. I will go into this more under the "young children" section, which follows.

Often the best thing to say is nothing. Just be with your children, hug them, be affectionate, and wait for them to speak. You can ask questions after an appropriate amount of time has passed, or later in the day or evening.

What about the way you physically act when your children have just failed and have been hit hard by it? This goes back to my original response: Always act supportive, loving, and understanding, and let the emotional condition of your child help guide your actions. This is a basic and supportive approach to responding to children's losses, and it can serve as a guideline for any loss or devastation in their lives.

In addition to these suggestions, there are three other variables to consider when you are attempting to help your children through emotionally difficult situations.

1. What are the ages of your children?
2. How open are you with your own emotions?
3. How do you usually act when your children fail?

Different Ages Have Different Needs
When determining how to respond to your children, it is always important to consider their age, out of respect for their unique needs. Young children have distinctly different needs from adolescents.

Young Children   Young children—kids from five to ten years of age—do not know how to appropriately deal with their emotions. They are too young to know even how to feel their real feelings, yet they are full of emotions and re-actions to life.

Let them know it is natural to feel strong emotions—anger, hurt, frustra-tion, fear—over failures and disappointing performances. The more they care about something, the more they have to lose—and it hurts. It can also feel hu-miliating or embarrassing to lose. Help them understand why they are react-ing, and that it is okay to feel and let go of their feelings. In fact, it is far better than holding the feelings inside themselves. And reassure them that you will not love them less if they should lose or fail in some way—no matter how badly. Reinforce to your child that love, especially yours, cannot be earned by anything they do. It is given freely, without strings, because you love them.

And when they feel disappointed, hurt, angry, or devastated by a loss, they need guidelines on how to act—and how to respond to their emotions. Talk to them about their actions and feelings, making sure they know there are ap-propriate ways to act and feel, both in the home and in public (such as avoid-ing public outbursts and dramatic displays of emotion). Give them boundaries.

You can explain to them that expressing their feelings to you or your spouse, or perhaps to their coach if they have one, is an effective way to work through their emotions so they can let go of them and move on to the next event or game. And perhaps most important, explain to them the value of looking for the positive things they achieved by just being in the competition.

Adolescents   Adolescents—kids from eleven years of age on into their late teens—have a greater capacity to feel their emotions than younger children. Yet, because their transition from childhood to adolescence is so sudden, they are psychologically unprepared to deal with the onslaught of emotions they are confronted with. Competitive athletic losses, disappointments, and fail-ures add to and intensify everything they are already feeling and can easily plunge them into confusing, moody, and often painful emotional states.

They may take on moods that can affect everyone around them—particu-larly you. Though adolescents can be difficult to talk to and deal with, when they become moody or emotionally reactive, behind this exterior lie pain and confusion. They do not know how to deal with any of it. Intense feelings scare them, making them feel out of control. This, very often, is the reason why they react so strongly.

Still, whatever their emotional reactions, it is far easier for you to reach out to your adolescent than it is for them to come to you. Sometimes the most dif-ficult thing for adolescents to admit is that they need help—that they need you. They desperately want their own identity, yet they have no idea how to find it. They need your help, but they do not always know how to ask for it.

This paradox puts them into a confusing and often lonely position. Understanding this—that sometimes they just cannot ask for your help, but often desperately need it—can make it easier to offer help when you feel it is appropriate.

A positive way to offer your help and support is to remind them that you are there for them if they ever need to talk. Your offer, even if they never take you up on it, will let them know you are available and willing to talk to them whenever they need you. This gives them the chance to have their independence and to come to you if necessary. It also gives them a certain measure of security, though it would be difficult for most of them to admit it.

There may be times when you feel it is appropriate to talk to your child about a particular disappointment or about their behavior, though they do not want to talk to you about it. You are still the parent. Sometimes you need to make the call and talk to them whether they like it or not. Remember, they still need you, and sometimes you may need to step in and help out with loving and caring intent. Obviously, if you use a controlling, know-it-all, demanding approach, you will only alienate them, pushing them further away from you.

How Emotionally Open Are You?

Your ability to respond to your children's emotional pains, confusion, and turmoil depends, to a large degree, upon how emotionally open you are. If you are willing to look honestly at your feelings and respond to them as best you can, not by suppressing them or explaining them away, you are automatically giving your children the message that you are emotionally available to them. You are creating a foundation for an emotional connection between you and them, which will help them more easily trust you emotionally as they grow older.

For example, even though all teens will emotionally close down to a certain degree, or entirely—out of fear, confusion, the inability to deal with their feelings, pain, etc.—they still need an emotional safety zone in their lives. Because you are their parent and the one they depend upon the most, you are the appropriate one to provide that zone. Adolescents need as much emotional security as possible—whether they would ever admit it or not. When they feel like they are bouncing off the emotional walls of their life, particularly after a painful athletic loss, you can be their anchor, ready and willing to be there for them. This does not guarantee they will take advantage of what you are willing to provide, but it does give them an emotional foundation to lean on and the choice to do so. In their lives, this will give them a much-needed safety zone.

If you are inexpressive and find that you have a tendency to avoid and suppress your emotions, it will be difficult for your children to approach you for emotional support. The message you are giving is, "I am uncomfortable with emotions." Even if they did come to you for help, there is going to be an inherent problem. First and most obvious, you will not have any working knowledge of how to talk to them about their emotions unless you are experienced in how to effectively respond to your own emotions. Logic and intellect alone are of no real help when it comes to dealing with feelings.

On the other hand, you do have a choice. You can change and learn how to become more responsive to your feelings. In time, you will discover that you will be able to relate with much more compassion and understanding to what your children are feeling, including when they are devastated by an athletic or any other kind of loss. Your increased sensitivity will give you greater insight into how you can be there for them—and offer an expanding emotional foundation for them to lean on.

You Can Always Learn More about Your Emotions

Whether you happen to be open, closed, or somewhere in the middle with your emotional awareness and sensitivity, you can always become more aware—and consequently, more sensitive. Emotional growth never ends unless you choose to stop it. And as you discover new emotional depths, releasing and healing constricted feelings you have been carrying, you automatically deepen your ability to love and to emotionally understand and relate to your children.

How do you emotionally grow to the next level, and then beyond that? The key, as with anything else, lies in your desire and willingness to follow through. Talking about learning how to better respond to your feelings is one thing, but the bottom line rests upon your follow-through. All change, whether small or large, begins with the choice to become different.

Most people do not want to put the effort into changing themselves—especially emotionally—whether they are parents or not. It takes commitment, time, courage, and the willingness to see and feel things hidden inside of you, things that for the most part you have been avoiding. Yet, because you are a parent, your motivation can be different from the motivation of those without children. Your children need you to be there for them when they face loss, hurt, and the pain they have to deal with in everyday life and as young athletes. You are the one they look to for support, help, and understanding, even if they will not admit to it. The more emotionally aware you become, the more you can give your children the words, safety, support, and understanding they need.

There are many different sections in this book that can help you become more emotionally aware, more connected with your children. Just by reading this book, you are giving yourself the opportunity to discover more about yourself and your relationship with your son or daughter. Many other books are also available, some of which I mention, that can be helpful. And, as discussed earlier, personal growth tapes, counseling, and other avenues are always available that offer valuable insight and direction on how to learn about your emotional self.

The best thing about it all is that you do not have to be perfect at anything you do, particularly when learning more about your emotional self. You just have to want to love your children as much as you can. When you do that, it is amazing how many answers can find their way to the surface.

Question 2—"In a year-round demanding sport, like swimming or gymnastics, there is a considerable time commitment, a lot of hard work, and often great disappointment. It takes tremendous effort physically, mentally, and emotionally for a young athlete to commit to this type of sport. Is all that effort worth it? Is it even healthy for a child to be in this type of demanding sport?"

Many parents wrestle with the answer to this question. It is a complex issue with several things to consider not only for your child, but for you also. Let us start with your children's needs. Then we will look at yours.

Children's Needs
All children have basic needs that cannot be met without their parents' help. Generally speaking, these basic needs are centered around the following: (1) survival, (2) security, (3) belonging, (4) self-esteem, (5) creativity and productivity, (6) the need to know, (7) a sense of aesthetics and balance in life, and (8) spirituality.

Children also have emotional needs, which always begin with the need to be loved—especially by their parents—and gradually expand toward the experience and expression of all other feelings. Family relationships, friendships, education, sports, and other such activities give children a chance to both discover and develop themselves, and begin learning how to meet their own needs. It is important for you to know their needs and to be able to help them meet them, for if they are not met, your children's development and growth will be debilitated. Their emotional state can be greatly constricted, and their abilities will be compromised.

It is not possible for children to avoid some emotional constriction and other problems as they grow up. Part of growing up is learning how to deal with difficulty, as well as learning the nature of responsibility.

Your Needs Are Important Too
Paying attention to, and meeting, your own needs is essential to your health, well-being, and ability to love your children. If you cannot do this, particu-

larly with your emotional needs, how can you be emotionally available to nurture and love a child?

Many parents sacrifice their own needs for their children's and then call it "unconditional love." This is a distorted concept of love. Parents do have to sacrifice their needs for their children sometimes, that is true, but they never have to sacrifice all their needs all the time. That is neither loving nor healthy—for parent or child. It gives the wrong message to children, that they are the center of the universe, and distorts their sense of value and expectation. And too many parents who have continually focused on just their children's needs end up resenting being a parent.

Perhaps the first step when looking at what is best for your children in the case of competitive sports is always to consider their needs and your needs. That way you can find a healthy balance.

Here is a list of questions. Take your time and think about the answers, using them as a guide. Then, whatever choice you make, you know you cared enough to think it out, both for you and your children.

❐ How do you really feel about giving that much time and energy?
❐ If the financial commitment is large, how does it affect your family budget?
❐ If you have other children, will your relationship with them be negatively affected by the time and energy you spend on this one child?
❐ Will your participation in the sport and all that entails create stress in your relationship with your spouse?
❐ Will you become so involved in the sport that it becomes the center of your life—of the family's life? And if it does, is that really okay with you?
❐ How long are you willing to commit to this?

You can probably think of a lot more questions, and it is important to do so. They will only help you further consider your needs. The key here is that you always have to be honest about how you and your spouse feel about taking on this level of responsibility. If you are not committed to this particular sport, and you support it anyway, you can end up resenting everything about it. That resentment will not only hurt you. It can end up hurting the relationship with your son or daughter, and eventually your entire family.

So, when looking at an athlete's time, emotional commitment, and hard work involved in a demanding competitive sport, be sure to look at what is involved for you. What if you decide you really do not want to commit to a sport that takes that much time and energy? Does that mean you are an unloving parent? No. It means you are an honest parent. Does it mean your child cannot participate? Not necessarily.

If you do not want to put the full amount of time and energy into the sport that is required, but you would like your child to be able to participate, explore your options. Perhaps you can share the time and energy needed with your spouse, and between the two of you, you can make it work. If it is a team sport maybe there are other people on the team who can help out with transportation, so that your time commitment and theirs will be lessened. Maybe you can talk to the coach and say, "This is what I can do. Is there a way it can work?" There are many ways things can be worked out so your child can still participate and you can meet your needs as well.

If you cannot find a way to allow your child to participate, or you feel the sport is not right for him or her, you need to explain why. Perhaps you simply cannot make the time commitment because of your work schedule, and there is no way around it. Maybe you are not able to meet the financial requirements of the sport. Perhaps your child is already involved in several other activities, and you do not have the time or energy to spread yourself any further. Whatever the reason or reasons, talk to your child about why you feel the way you do.

Potential Drawbacks and Benefits of a Demanding Sport

What if you have looked at the time, energy, and financial commitment, and you decide that if your child really wants to do this sport you would be willing to support him or her? It may be a stretch, but you are willing. What is the next step? Now you look at the opportunities the sport itself presents. There are two sides to consider. The more demanding the sport, the more reasons you can find not to be involved. At the same time, because of the very nature of the sport's demands, there are worthwhile reasons to participate.

Here is a list of what can be potential negatives and positives, for the more demanding sports. Add whatever reasons you may have to the list. The point is to help you look at the merits of the sport.

The Potential Drawbacks

1. The time commitment to the sport is so great that it prevents a child/teen from participating in other activities, such as school dances, parties, and trips. Consequently, they do not have a chance to experience the variety of things available that are a valuable and fun part of growing up.

2. The athletes are often physically, mentally, and emotionally spent because the workouts are so strenuous. They often have trouble keeping up with their homework. Beyond that, many nights they cannot get enough hours of sleep to properly rest themselves.

3. Athletes feel limited as to who their friends can be, because there is not enough time—with homework, workouts, and competitions— to allow for any free time with nonathlete friends.

4. There is not enough family time. All of a young athlete's time is spent training, going to school, eating, doing homework, and sleeping. Parents and children spend little time talking to each other. A parent's responsibility often ends up revolving around supplying food, transportation, a bed, money, and domestic service.

5. Young athletes are not able to develop and practice any social skills in the real world. They are isolated in their own small world of the sport.

6. Sometimes a coach ends up spending more time with a child/teen than do his or her their own parents. Because of this, that coach can sometimes have more influence over the boy or girl than their own mother and father.

7. There never seems to be any time for a child/teen to have to himself or herself.

The Potential Benefits

1. The commitment to something difficult, such as a year-round competitive sport, gives young athletes a greater opportunity to develop their sense of determination, will, character, and other inner strengths that are so necessary for success.

2. When athletes commit to a demanding sport that asks so much of their time and energy, they place themselves in a position of risk. Somewhere along the way they are going to fail—in some aspect of a sport. There is always the potential for humiliation, rejection, pain, hurt, and disappointment in any failure. But in a supportive atmosphere—created by a coach, parents, teammates and friends—surviving the failure becomes a valuable life experience. They can learn that failing does not mean they are a failure as a person, and that their value to their parents, coach, teammates, and friends does not depend upon their performance as an athlete.

3. Athletes feel like they are a part of something bigger than themselves when so much of their lives revolve around a sport that is year-round. Participating in that sport becomes a way of life. Because of this intense focus, athletes can develop a sense of belonging—and a place where they belong—which is a basic human need for all of us, particularly for young people.

4. When athletes are committed, disciplined, and have the will and determination to go to all the workouts, competitions, meetings, and travel trips that are required for a year-round sport, they gain a sense of accomplishment in what they are doing. Their commitment, because of its challenging nature, bonds the athletes even more to the sport, as well as to their teammates who share the same commit-

ment. Their ability to stay committed also gives them a sense of confidence because they are capable of accomplishing what they set out to do in their lives.

5. There is a depth of friendship available in demanding sports. Teammates are all facing the same difficult challenges, and by doing it together there is a natural bonding process. In many cases, their friends—who often become part of an extended family—are the major reason they stay in the sport.

6. A demanding sport asks for a high level of responsibility from the athletes. They have to learn how to discipline and organize themselves around their homework, workouts, time off, family responsibilities, and competitions. Their ability to do this teaches them valuable skills that will benefit them in their current day-to-day activities, as well as in their adult life.

7. The physical training of a demanding sport conditions and develops young athletes' bodies and allows for their participation in a healthy activity.

8. Being part of a year-round sport offers young athletes a safe, supervised, healthy atmosphere to share with friends.

9. A skilled and nurturing coach can often offer direction and advice to young athletes concerning their life choices. Many coaches end up becoming extremely positive influences in a young athlete's life. Often with rebellious young kids, it is the coach, not the parent, who can keep an athlete from going in the wrong direction. And in dysfunctional or troubled family situations, the coach is very often the only safe, trusted, and positive influence in a young athlete's life. Many athletes, whether from positive or dysfunctional families, stay in contact with their coaches for years after retiring from the sport.

10. A demanding sport can offer young people a chance to experience a sense of passion in their lives. So many kids have no way to tap into anything in their school experience that offers them an opportunity to feel passionate about something.

11. With so many school districts doing away with athletics, music, and art, there are far less creative avenues for young people to pursue. Depending upon the program, year-round sports can be fun, healthy, and extremely creative, particularly in the development of an athlete's Whole Self.

These are some of the potential negatives and positives in demanding, competitive sports, which generally are year-round in nature. Obviously, not all programs or coaches will fit the positives on the list. No program or coach is perfect. The key here is to decide for yourself. What feels right? Then, decide what you and your son or daughter together, like—and dislike—about a program, a coach, and the many other aspects of what is being offered.

The right program can offer a great deal to your child or teen. There are many positives and benefits to be gained from being involved in a year-round sport. At the same time, some programs can be far more negative than positive to a young person. This can occur when there is too much emphasis on performance and minimal attention to the development of the Whole Self. It also occurs when a coach is very controlling, dominating, and abusive to kids. If young athletes are being shamed, humiliated, and hurt, there is something very wrong with the way they are being coached. This is not a positive program, no matter how "successful" your child might become under this coach.

If you decide to join a particular program there are still things to consider, for some situations are unknown until you have the opportunity to experience them. In any program, it is important to consider the impact the other athletes have upon your child or teen. Sometimes certain athletes are not desirable for your son or daughter to be around. They can be too competitive, pushy, arrogant, or dominating for your taste. Or they may be too cliquish, excluding your child from friendships. In some cases, the entire clique can be resentful of your child's success, or then hurtful and judgmental over his or her lack of it.

Also, how do you feel about the other parents in the program? How comfortable are you when you are around them? Are they too competitive with each other or with you? Are they considerate and enjoyable to be around? Do you share common values? They do not all have to fit your comfort zone, but remember that you are going to be spending considerable time around them.

In short, be careful who you trust with your children. Check out coaches and programs, and do not be afraid to leave a program if you feel it is not in your child's—or your—best interest. On the whole, coaches try their best and give their all, and the vast majority of them and their programs offer a positive and supportive experience for a young athlete. The coaches I know choose coaching as a way of life; it is not just a job. They are totally committed to their kids, and they genuinely care about them. They are also human and have their imperfections, but they are usually always willing to talk to and work with parents, as well as their children, doing whatever they can to be a better coach.

Sometimes it takes effort and time for parents, coaches, and athletes to learn to work with each other. Sometimes everything works from the very beginning. Because demanding sports are so challenging, they can easily bring up conflicts and emotions, sometimes for all parties concerned.

Look for balance. Learning to find it is all part of the experience of being involved in the sport.

Question 3—"I have one child who, as an athlete and student, always tries his best; and another who doesn't seem to care. How do I help motivate the second one?"

It is a confusing situation if you do not understand why one child chooses to be less motivated. Often, on the surface at least, there appears to be no logical reason for it. But if you look beneath the surface, you can usually find one.

First, look at the problems your less-motivated child might be experiencing in his or her life—with a sibling, with school, with friends, with a coach or sport, or with you or your spouse. Any such problem can potentially cause depression, anger, self-pity, fear, and other constricting emotions that can lead to a lack of motivation. See if you can get your child to talk to you about how he or she is feeling. And then help them address the problem.

For the most part you are probably already doing this, but that does not mean you are seeing what is really going on. That may be because you are seeing with your intellect only, not with your feelings. You are missing the emotional part of the problem. Or maybe you do understand the emotional problem, but it still does not seem to explain the lack of motivation. At this point, look beyond the more obvious indicators. Keep them in mind, for they are still indicators, but look deeper for the larger picture. There is always a larger picture.

There are two areas that can be extremely helpful in understanding behavior patterns. Two areas may not sound like very many, but they are significant enough for several books to have been written on each area. Though it is impossible to offer absolute answers when it comes to human nature, these particular areas do offer tremendous insight that can greatly expand your understanding of your child's behavior, not to mention your own.

First, there is the birth order of the child/teen to consider. A noticeable pattern of behavior can be identified with the order in which one is born. It is not a hard and fast rule that every child will follow the pattern, but with the athletes and parents I have worked with, the patterns have been very consistent.

Secondly, all children develop their own very unique personalities. According to the Enneagram, which I have found to be a very useful tool in understanding personality development, there are nine distinctly different personality types. Whatever type your child is will play a significant role in how he or she behaves.

An important thing to keep in mind is that birth order and personality types most certainly influence people. Though there are other influences, such as how parents treat their children, divorces, deaths, diseases, and other significant issues that affect children and teens, it is extremely helpful to understand the significance of birth order and personality types.

The Influences of Birth Order

When looking at motivation, behavior, will, responsibility, etc. in young athletes, one of the first things to consider is the birth order of the children or teens involved. There is a specific and unique psychological impact felt by children when they are born first, second, third, fourth, and so on. This leads to patterns of behavior as to how each child approaches life. Being aware of birth order, and its effects, can be remarkably helpful in understanding why people of any age act the way they do.

What follows is a very brief look at the characteristics of the different birth orders. It would be valuable if you took the time to read a specific book on it. The book used here as a reference is by Kevin Leman, titled *The Birth Order Book*.

Firstborn With firstborns, you can have two basic types of people: compliant and wanting to please, or strong-willed and aggressive. Both are trying to live up to being the "firstborn." The compliant one is often the perfect child, always trying to please their parents. The strong-willed one is usually highly competitive, whether it be in sports, school, or anything else. Both are often called perfectionists. Both types are trying to get recognition, approval, and acknowledgment—ultimately love, a parent's love.

Firstborns feel the burden of being the first child in the family. They are the oldest. They usually feel a sense of obligation to succeed, to realize their parents' dreams. For so many, life itself can often feel like it is about duty and obligation.

The oldest most often feels responsible for setting an example for all other siblings that follow. They lead, because dad and mom are counting on them to set an example. They are typically very responsible, often driven to succeed. They can easily end up resenting the responsibility, but they do it anyway. It is their nature. However, in some cases, they do just the opposite of everything just suggested—rebelling against the weight of responsibility.

Middle Child "Middle child" usually refers to the second child born out of three children. Yet a child can be born the third of four, the fourth of five, and so on, and still have the behavior of a second child. The determining factor in being a middle child is that there is someone born before and after.

When children are born in the middle, whether second in order or later, they determine their behavior by watching the firstborn or the child ahead of them. They figure out how to act so that they will not live in the shadow of their older sibling, though they often do. They want to stand out, to get their parents' attention—to get their love. What you will see the most with middle children is that they will do just the opposite of the first child or the child just ahead of them. In fact, if you are going to choose a word that best describes middle children, it would be "contradictory."

For example, I have seen many second-born athletes take over the first-born's role of responsibility, success, and competitiveness when the firstborn chose to rebel against the burden of responsibility. This was the second-born's way of competing with the child ahead of him. If you did not know their ages, you would think the second-born was the firstborn. And many of these rebelling firstborns look up to their younger siblings, even lean on them for support. They know who is most responsible.

Having said that, middle children are also the most difficult to define, generalize about, and describe. As opposite as they want to be, they can also choose to be similar in some ways. It all depends upon how they perceive the actions and personality of the child ahead of them.

In sports, for instance, it is common to see second-born children follow their brothers and sisters into the same sport. As far apart as they may be in personalities, they still look up to their older siblings, often idolizing them. At the same time, of the second-borns who follow their brothers or sisters into the same sport, you will find some being just as competitive and others being far less competitive. There is no norm—other than contradiction.

If you are feeling just a bit confused as to how to look at second-borns, join the crowd. Nearly all who study birth order feel the same way—middle children can be a mystery to define. Some will do this, and then some will do that. Perhaps the first and easiest way to look at them is through their need to do the opposite—their need to stand out. Though they can often "follow in the footsteps" in certain areas, they will usually do the opposite in everything else.

There is one more thing to add when speaking of a second-born. If the second-born is the opposite sex from the first child, they become the "firstborn" of their gender. They usually end up feeling the weight and responsibility of being the firstborn as much as the *actual* firstborn. The pressures of having to succeed can weigh just as heavily upon them as they do on their older sibling.

Second-Born/Same Sex A second child of the same sex as the firstborn faces an additional burden. They are, in one way or another, always compared to their older sibling. This can be especially true in sports when both siblings are athletes. The second child's talent and performances are always being compared to the first child's—by coaches, other athletes, other parents, often by their own mothers and fathers, but mostly by themselves. Worse yet, if these same-sex second-borns fall short of talent and achievement, they nearly always feel the onus of failing to be "as good" as their older siblings. Yet, on the other side of it, if they turn out to be better athletes, they feel like they are hurting their older siblings—who they have always looked up to.

Last-Born The last-born, regardless of sex, is usually called "the baby"—they even refer to *themselves* as the baby. They too are competing for their parents' attention and love. The problem is that others got a head start on getting mom and dad's attention. In many families, the parents pay less attention to the last-borns compared to those ahead of them. They have already raised two or three kids. Often, it is the older siblings who do much of the parenting for last-borns.

Last-borns are known for being the clowns and the rebels, and for being somewhat unpredictable and independent. They live with a certain ambivalence, being made fun of and put down one minute, the next minute being treated as if they are special because they are the youngest. The last-born will always be unique—and make sure everyone knows it.

The first big clue as to why some children may not be as motivated as their siblings lies in birth order, particularly when it comes to middle children. It is not the only clue, but it is always worth considering when trying to understand your children's motivations—or lack of them.

Personality Types and the Enneagram

As mentioned earlier, I have found great value in referring to the Enneagram to understand personality development. The Enneagram is a framework, a way of looking at and understanding human nature and the nine different personality types it describes. It is an insightful and very accurate resource for explaining certain motivations we all have.

The Enneagram has been in written form for about 2,500 years, beginning with the Sufis, though its origins probably go back thousands more years. Several authors offer detailed information on the Enneagram. Though they will give you slightly different perspectives, all have done their own research and have added to what the Sufis contributed.

It is important to keep in mind that even with all that is currently known, we will always be discovering new insight into our personalities. We are far too complex and intricate to ever fully understand ourselves. Yet, the considerable information that is available in the books on the Enneagram can give you valuable insight that, as a parent, can prove extremely helpful.

All children—all people—develop their own personalities. The early stages of development begin around two to three years of age. The type of personality a child develops will be based upon the relationship they form with their parents.

Children's worlds center around themselves and their parents. Their need is so great for their parents' love that they focus a great deal of their energy on getting it. It is their parents' love—physical and emotional attention, security, approval, and acknowledgment—that makes children feel safe. Any form of stress, turmoil, anger, conflict, or unhappiness that they see in their parents threatens their safety and security, which is closely tied to their sense of survival. Added to this is the feeling that *they* are the reason for the stress, because as children, they see themselves as the center of the world. To avoid the risk of not being loved, of not being wanted, they adapt themselves to act in ways that they think will earn their parents' love.

As they adapt to what their parents present them with, they create a way of being, of relating to them. This becomes the foundation of their personality type. They continue to build upon this foundation, bringing it into their relationships with their siblings, if they have any, and then out into the greater world, beyond immediate family.

Their personality type, so pivotal to how they relate to everything and everyone in their world, is often overlooked as to its importance. It is, in reality, central to everything they do in their lives, influencing how they act, think, and feel. It is the driving force within them.

Look at certain people—athletes and nonathletes—that stand out to you. There is always something about them that clearly defines them, that sets them apart from others. Some are natural leaders. Others have an uncanny ability to be peacemakers. Certain people seem to be able to achieve whatever they want, often with little effort. Nothing seems beyond them. Others can light up whatever room they happen to walk into. They are like a light drawing energy to them. And others, like Mother Teresa, nurture in a way that can gain worldwide attention.

The more you understand your child/teen's personality type—as well as your own, because you are seeing them through the eyes of *your* personality type—the more understandable their behavior, feelings, and motivations can be. Over the years numerous parents have told me of the tremendous value that understanding personality types has been to them and their families.

It is not possible to explain in detail the nine different personality types, for it would require a book in itself to do so, and that is not this book's major focus. But it is worth mentioning them in regard to the question of why some young athletes are more motivated than others. Understanding your child's personality, especially when taken into consideration with their birth order, can help you gain a much deeper insight into their motivations.

Here is a brief look at the highlights of the different personality types. This list does not begin to represent their full complexity and intricacy, but it will give you a sense of what they are like.

Keep in mind that each type always has healthy and unhealthy characteristics, just as each has its strengths and vulnerabilities. Also, the names of the personalities can vary according to different authors, yet all authors do follow the same numbering system so that, regardless of the name, the numbers all correlate. The following list is taken from Don Riso's *Personality Types*.

One—The Reformer: rational, principled, orderly, perfectionistic
Two—The Helper: caring, generous, possessive, manipulative

Three—The Motivator: self-assured, competitive, narcissistic, hostile
Four—The Artist: creative, intuitive, introverted, depressive
Five—The Thinker: perceptive, analytic, eccentric, paranoid
Six—The Loyalist: likable, dutiful, dependent, masochistic
Seven—The Generalist: accomplished, impulsive, excessive, manic
Eight—The Leader: self-confident, forceful, dominating, combative
Nine—The Peacemaker: receptive, reassuring, passive, neglectful

Some children develop personality traits that stand out early in their lives, while other children's traits may emerge more strongly later in their lives. Yet, if you know what to look for, there are usually signs early on that can give you clues as to which type your child is.

Here is an example of how personality types can influence how parents can perceive their child.

We were talking about achievement, how important it was to parents, and how sometimes it became too important, often blinding them to the truer nature of their children. One mother, who was sitting in the middle of the room, raised her hand.

"I cannot figure out why my son does not achieve more," she began. "He has everything he needs—strength, size, training, even a strong will—but he just doesn't seem to be able to put it all together."

"What do you mean—put it all together?" I asked.

"Well, he has mediocre performances," she replied. "I know he can do more, but I don't know what the missing ingredient is."

As she was speaking, I wondered why she was so focused on his performance. She had not mentioned what he was achieving, just what he was not achieving.

"Can I ask you something?" I said. "Are you pretty successful at the things you do in your life?"

She laughed, somewhat taken aback by my question, and said, in a self-deprecating way, "Well, I do okay, I guess."

"Do you find that success comes easy to you?" I asked. "I know that you have to work for it, but when you do, do you always seem to be successful?"

After hesitating, she finally said, "Yes, it does seem to work that way."

"When you see others struggle with their jobs and financial issues do you wonder why—because it always seems so easy for you?" I asked.

She hesitated again, this time a little longer, then, "I have always wondered about that."

"I'm asking you these questions so I can learn more about your personality type," I said. "You sound like you might be what I refer to as the Achiever—the "three" in the Enneagram. The type three achieves in life at a very high level. And it seems to be easy for them. It's as if they have a talent for achieving whatever they want. When they go after something, they usually always get it. That sounds a lot like you. What do you think?"

She was thoughtful for a moment, and then said, "I would agree, that does sound like me, though it feels a little awkward to talk about it."

"You are not bragging or anything. I know that. That is just how it is for you. It is very helpful to know—and understand—your personality type, since you see your world through it—including your son. Your ease at achieving success can present a real problem for you when you try to understand your son's apparent lack of success. The problem is, you can't understand it."

"You're right—I can't," she said, laughing. "That's why I asked you."

"When you look at him," I began, "you are looking through your eyes, using your framework for achieving success. The assumption in your framework is that all he has to do is apply himself and everything will fall into place—like it does for you—and he will achieve what he goes after."

"That is my assumption, now that I think about it," she said. "I always wonder what's wrong. He seems to be doing everything right, but he just can't seem to get there. I try to help him, but nothing I do seems to help."

"Perhaps it would help if you looked at what you think success is. Do you think it is based upon how much you achieve?"

"Well…yes. Isn't it pretty much that way, especially for athletes?"

"In many ways, yes," I answered. "But there are different ways to look at achievement. You look at it in terms of tangible results, right?"

"Yes, I'd say so."

"That is certainly valid," I said. "Especially when your personality is so focused on achievement. But what about your son's personality type? His does not appear to be the same as yours. He will still value achievement, but not in the same way you do. He may be applying himself with the same commitment you would have, but the results he is achieving are in different areas, such as learning about the power of his will by the way he works out, being a good friend to his teammates, learning that he is not defined by his achievements, and other such things. His framework of value systems is different from yours, and he may be looking for different things in life than you are. In fact, the things he is learning can be valuable life lessons that he can carry with him way beyond his sport."

"You know," she said, "I think you are right, but it's still real hard for me to not see his lack of success—in the obvious areas."

"It will be difficult for you," I said. "You are an achiever. Achievement is what you focus on—and value highly. But that is not all of who you are. You can also learn to appreciate that your son is achieving, maybe not in your terms, but perhaps in his, even though it may not be obvious to you. Maybe you have never really looked at what he might be learning. Would you be willing to let him find his own way, looking for the things he is achieving, without thinking that somehow he is failing?"

"Yes. When you put it like that, of course I am willing. I love him."

"There is one other thing you might consider. How do you know that he is not achieving more so he will not have to live up to your success? I am not saying he is doing this. But he could be. Maybe, in his eyes, you are not such an easy act to follow. Besides, he knows how you see him. How do you think he feels about your feeling that he just can't seem to put it all together? "

She was silent, shaking her head. "He is probably hurt by it," she said.

"Why don't you talk to him?" I said. "Tell him what you have become aware of, and how much you love him. Ask him to share with you what his sports experience is like, what he gets out of it, and what he is learning. You may open up a whole new relationship, and a much greater sense of appreciation for what he has been doing."

"I think that's a good idea," she said.

"And remember," I added, "your son is young. Whatever he is doing now is not necessarily an indicator of who he will become, or what he will ultimately achieve."

"I am already beginning to understand that," she said, smiling.

A Final Note

Young athletes face a very competitive world and unique pressures day after day, especially when they have an athletic sibling. As you look at the question of their motivation, you can only try to understand it as best as you can, knowing there is always more to learn. If your child is less motivated to achieve than his or her sibling, certainly try to find out why, reminding yourself that children often have reasons why they hold back—often to get your attention. They are trying to find their niche, their identity, to establish themselves in the family and in your eyes.

Learning about birth order and personality types, and paying attention to such things as problems at school, conflicts in friendships, relationships with their siblings, difficulties in their sport, and most certainly how you treat them will be an immense help in understanding your children's motivations. As a parent, you want to help motivate your children when you see them lagging behind, giving up, or holding back—whether they are young athletes or not. Yet, there is no right answer at any given time as to what you should say or do. It all depends upon the situation, how they are feeling, how you are feeling, what athletic failures they have already had, how good an athlete their sibling is, and so on. It is complex, and perhaps you are never going to consistently get it right. Yet, there are some things you can always fall back on. They want you to love them, to pay attention to them. They want to be acknowledged for who they are. They do not want to be mixed in and lost among a crowd of brothers and sisters. They do not want to be seen as an "athlete." They want to be recognized as a person.

With this in mind, remember to talk to your children—with your heart, with understanding and patience. This demonstrates that you see them as people who matter to you. Even if they do not want to respond, do not give up. Look for problems they may be facing in their lives, with their friends, at school, or with their sport. Ask them how they feel about the way you treat them. Talk to them about how they treat you. Also talk to them about how they feel about being the oldest, the second, or third child. See what pressures, responsibilities, or comparisons they might be feeling. Ask them how your actions might be contributing to these feelings.

These are the kinds of things that help children and teens with their motivation. Consistent, positive attention and support can have an amazing effect upon a child's attitude—in competitive sports as well as everywhere else

As you probably already know, none of what is suggested here can guarantee that your children will be more motivated; there are no guarantees. But working with this information and gaining the insights and understanding that will be derived from it will create a very solid, nurturing foundation that can make it clear how much you want to understand and love them, which ultimately is perhaps the most effective way to help create positive motivation.

Question 4—"How can I be involved in my children's sport without putting unwanted pressure on them?"

Many parents believe that just their presence at an athletic event can often cause their children to feel a certain degree of additional pressure. And they are right.

Without question, your children care how you feel about their achievements—or lack of them. They know what you expect and want. They are aware of how you react to their competitions, and they do not want to disappoint you, even if you tell them you will not be disappointed. No matter how much they might deny it, how you react always matters to them.

So how do you as a parent involve yourself in your children's sport without causing any unwanted pressure? There are different answers for different families because the relationships between parents and children are unique to each family. So the best way to answer this is first to give you a framework to help you assess your own situation and then follow that up with specific guidelines to help you act accordingly.

The first question to consider is what causes the pressure—the fear—that young athletes feel. All young athletes feel varying degrees of fear when they compete. Some fear comes from wanting to do well for their coach or teammates. Other fears can come from the expectations they put upon themselves. Then there are brothers and sisters to live up to, and championships to compete in. There is the fear of failure—and the fear of success. And of course there is the fear of disappointing a parent.

The greatest fear that the majority of young athletes feel centers on the relationship with their parents. They fear many things, such as disappointing them, not living up to their expectations, being rejected, being shamed and humiliated, failing to succeed, failing to make up for all the time and money invested in them and their sport, and so on. There are very real reasons why children and adolescents feel so much fear. The more you understand these reasons, not just intellectually but with an emotional awareness as well, the wiser you can be when it comes to participating in your children's activities in a way that creates the least amount of fear for them.

Let us start by taking a look at why children are so concerned about how their parents feel about them. There are certain core issues that all children have in common. And not surprisingly, they all revolve around the issue of love.

A Parent's Love Represents Safety and Security

There is an inherent need for safety and security that infants and very young children look to you to provide. Their primary needs are, at the very least, food, shelter, and clothing. But far more importantly, it is your love and the way you express that love that is the real key to their sense of safety and security. They need your love to emotionally survive. Anything that threatens their feeling of being loved also threatens their safety and security. For example, if you are very angry, hurt, or upset for some reason—whether it is aimed at them or not—they will feel to some degree threatened, because anything that disturbs your emotional stability affects how you relate to them.

When children reach the age where they can participate in activities independently of you—school, sports, music, dance, etc.—they are beginning the process of learning to take greater responsibility for themselves. This does not diminish their need for your love, approval, and acceptance. They are extremely vulnerable to the outside world. You are still their parent. Your love and approval still represents safety, security, and a form of protection.

When your children become involved in competitive sports, as opposed to recreational sports, they face even greater responsibilities, such as learning to be more disciplined, dealing with a higher level of competition and comparison, risking potential rejection and judgment, and fitting in with the other athletes. Their need to lean on you for their safety and security becomes even more important, for they are still too young to provide it for themselves.

Even as they grow into adolescents, your children still need your approval, support, understanding, and love. These things provide them with a safety net when something goes askew in their world.

How you love your children—your actions, words, tone of voice, attention, and emotional understanding of them—is the most significant way you can provide a sense of safety and security.

Children Fear the Loss of Your Love

Parents, or one particular parent, are the original source of love for infants—which also makes them the original source of safety, security, and survival. Because infants have an emotional dependency on their parents' love and nurturing, they develop an equally strong fear of its loss. The loss of a parent's love creates a feeling of separation, and that creates pain. This dynamic—the need for love and the fear of its loss—is so central in an infant's life that it becomes an integral part of its emotional makeup.

As an infant grows into a child, and then into adolescence, the need for a parent's love—and the fear of its loss—still remains part of the subconscious.

The Subconscious Reacts to Any Potential Loss of Love

Your subconscious monitors everything in your life. It tries to provide you with what you think you need to survive—to be happy, to have love in your life, and so on. It takes its cues for what you need from your beliefs about survival, happiness, and love. It then interprets information as it comes in, to see if your needs are being provided for. If you think you need something to survive, your subconscious does everything it can to provide you with that something.

In the case of an infant, the subconscious knows that infant needs its parents' love to survive, to feel safe and secure. It becomes a lookout, so to speak, always scanning, "Is the love still there? Is everything okay? Do they still love me?" The subconscious is watching for any potential threat to the parents' love.

When there is a threat the subconscious sounds the alarm, causing an immediate reaction of fear in that infant. The need for a parent's love becomes so deeply embedded in the subconscious—because it is linked to basic survival—that no matter how well a parent loves that infant, it will not be enough to stop the subconscious from continually scanning for what could go wrong. It knows that no matter how much love is given, if that love ever stops, the infant's safety, security, and survival are immediately threatened.

If you take this further and look at what happens when that infant becomes a child and then an adolescent, you will see that the original fear of loss of love still remains. The infant, child, and adolescent—and the adult for that matter—all share the same subconscious, and it continues to give the original message—a parent's love is needed to survive—until that message is changed. And that does not happen before adulthood, when one has had enough experience in life to develop a stable sense of self-love, confidence, and emotional depth. Until this happens, children and adolescents will be vulnerable to any real or perceived threat to their parents' love.

Perceived—and Real—Fear of Losing a Parent's Love

The fear of loss of love that children and adolescents feel is a natural part of them. Any threat—perceived or real—to your love can invoke a reaction from them. A "threat" refers to the nature of your actions when you are around your children. A real threat is a form of personal rejection. A perceived threat is not a personal rejection, but might be perceived as such by your child.

Examples of real threats:

- You give the most approval to your children when they achieve at a high level, indicating your disapproval of low achievement.
- You raise your voice or outright yell at them if they fail or do not try hard enough to suit you.
- Your tone of voice communicates your disappointment and disapproval whenever they fail to live up to your expectations.
- You believe your success as a parent rides upon your children's achievements.
- You correct them in a way that makes them feel like they can never do it right.
- You continually criticize them.
- You do not seem to have enough time to participate with your children in their activities.
- There is a divorce in the family.
- You do not understand or relate to how your children feel.
- You do not talk to them on an emotional level.
- You always have to be right when you communicate with your children.
- You "blow up" when angry.
- You are a controlling parent.
- You continually remind your children how much money their activities are costing you.
- You act as though you are a victim of life, focusing on your own problems.

The examples just listed are actions that could be considered real threats to your children concerning the security of your love. All of these situations can create some form of pressure (fear of rejection) for them, the feeling that they had better not displease you, or the belief that they have to make up for your failures—real or perceived—in life. Whether you mean it that way or not, your children can easily see it that way.

Perceived threats, as opposed to real threats, can be obvious or subtle. Here are several different situations that can create a perceived threat:

- You are disappointed in what has happened to your children—as opposed to being disappointed in them personally—but all they see is your disappointment, and they take it personally.
- You are upset at something in your life other than your children—your

> spouse, your job, etc.—and your focus is on your frustration rather than on your children.
>
> ❒ You pay more attention to another sibling. This can be a real or perceived threat depending upon how it is done.
>
> ❒ Your topic of conversation is usually about your children's achievements. This tells them how important you think performance is.

Real or perceived threats to your love for them are what will scare your children the most. Either type of threat can cause a painful feeling of separation from you. Your willingness to understand and to be sensitive to their fears—to all their emotions—is essential in helping you recognize when they are feeling threatened.

Emotional Awareness — The Key to Knowing How to Participate with Your Children

Children and adolescents are complex and intricate, especially emotionally. And while it may be easy to understand why a child or adolescent has so many fears and why your love is so important to them, it sometimes can be far more difficult to relate to what they are actually feeling.

It is important to have an emotional awareness, as well as an intellectual understanding, to be able to accurately perceive a young person's needs with depth and wisdom. The problem you usually face in being able to do this is that as an adult, you are looking through your eyes, through your history, through your emotional scars, trying to understand how a child or teen feels. It can be difficult enough to accurately understand your own feelings, let alone another's, particularly when you are looking through your own filters.

If you have not healed your emotional scars and have suppressed painful and uncomfortable feelings as a way to deal with your past, you will create a certain degree of numbness around your emotions. To whatever degree you have emotionally numbed yourself, that will be the degree to which you cannot emotionally relate to, nor understand, your children—or anyone else. It will be as if parts of them are invisible to you.

Here is an example of the effect that an emotionally closed parent can have upon her child:

> The girl raised her hand, but she seemed reluctant to ask her question. She was thirteen, tall and thin, with long dark hair.
>
> "What's on your mind?" I asked, trying to make it easier for her.
>
> Her hands were shaking. She said nothing for a while.
>
> "I wonder if you could help me with something," she said. "I can't stop my knees from shaking before my races."
>
> "What do you think you are afraid of?" I asked.

"Nothing," she said quickly. "They just shake and I want to stop them."

"Well . . . okay," I said. "Can I ask you something?"

"Okay."

"What's wrong with your knees shaking?" I asked. "They are just knees, and a lot of athletes' knees shake before their races. For most, it is normal anxiety because they don't know what is going to happen, and the race is important to them."

She was silent for awhile. "It embarrasses me," she said.

"Do you think people will judge you?" I asked.

"I don't know," she answered. "Maybe."

"Do you think it's okay that you might feel afraid?"

"I try not to feel afraid."

"But are you, maybe just a little?" I said. "It would certainly be normal if your were."

With her hands still shaking, she said, "Well maybe just a little, I think."

"What do you think you are afraid of?"

"I don't know . . ."

"What about your parents, or your coach or teammates," I asked. "Do you have any fear of disappointing any of them?"

She was quiet, then said, "Maybe my parents."

"Well that's understandable," I told her. "It's pretty common to not want to disappoint your parents. Have you ever talked them about your fears?"

"Not really," she said, softly.

"Maybe you could now," I said. "After the seminar, could you go home and share with them what we talked about? That could open the door to them understanding you more, and making it a little easier for you. They don't want you to feel afraid."

"I don't know . . . maybe," she said.

"Okay," I said. "If you can, it might help. Now, as far as your knees go, the next time you feel them shake before a race, try talking to them silently in your mind. Tell them they can shake all they want—it's okay with you. And if they continue shaking, you just let them—all they want. It won't hurt you. They will get tired of shaking after awhile. When you let something be okay, you might be amazed at how it can just go away. And as far as being embarrassed about them, if anyone asks about your knees or makes a comment, you tell them they are in training, that your knees shake when they are warming up before your races. Try it and see what happens. Remember. It's okay if they shake."

She smiled and said, "Okay. Thanks."

That night I met her mother, who approached me, said hello, and then asked if her daughter had spoken during the seminar.

"Yes, she did, as a matter of fact," I said. "Can I ask, how close to your daughter are you?"

"Oh, we are very close," she answered.

"I think she is feeling a lot of fear," I said.

The mother was clearly surprised. "My daughter doesn't feel any fear," she said, laughing and shaking her head. "She is very confident—always has been."

"I think she is presenting a false sense of confidence to you—and to the world," I said. "I sensed that she was very afraid when we spoke today."

"That's just not true," she said. "My daughter is confident." The mother laughed again, shaking her head at the absurdity of my comments.

I tried once more. "She seems to be afraid of disappointing you and your husband," I said.

"She knows we won't be disappointed," she said, once again shaking her head and smiling. "Our family is very close. No, everything's fine with her—it always is."

"Okay," I said. And that was as far as the conversation went.

There was no doubt in my mind that the mother cared very much for her daughter. That was clear. What was also clear was that she failed to relate to her emotionally. She did not and would not consider even the possibility that her daughter might be frightened. She had an image of her, and that was who her daughter was. Feelings did not enter into it.

Had the mother been more emotionally aware she could have accurately sensed what her daughter was really feeling, rather than just assume what she was feeling. It would have made it possible for her to go to her daughter and talk with her, to reassure her that she would not be disappointed in her if she should fail. Instead the mother chose to hang onto an image of her daughter that she wanted to believe—whether it was true or not—and in the process emotionally shut her daughter out even further.

Hundreds of conversations I have had with fathers and mothers have been remarkably similar to this story. Some parents have been so emotionally closed down, so unaware of what their children were feeling, that when I spoke to their children about their feelings and then to the parents about their perceptions of what their children were feeling, the conversations could have been about two different families.

The value of being or becoming emotionally aware is so high, it cannot be expressed strongly enough. If you want to avoid putting unwanted pressure on your children, become as emotionally aware as you can, for it will help you to recognize when your kids are feeling pressure. Then you can do something about it.

Your emotional awareness is the most valuable, internal monitoring system you have available to you. Whatever level of emotional awareness you currently have, from very little to quite a bit, you can always expand it. Learning about your emotions is an ongoing process of discovery that takes time and attention—and never ends. Yet, whatever it takes is well worth it, for it will only enhance your ability to relate to and love your children.

Having Guidelines to Monitor Your Involvement in Your Children's Sports
It is wise to set up specific guidelines around your involvement in your children's sports. It is an invaluable way to gain greater insight into their emotional state and to let them know you respect their feelings. These guidelines are not rigid. They are meant to be modified and added to as your emotional awareness grows and your children's needs change. Over time, and with practice and patience, they will help you build a foundation of communication with your children that can serve you for years.

It is important to remember that, ultimately, what will make your guidelines work is your love. And it is the very strength of your love that will allow you and your children to survive the mistakes you are sure to make.

Expand Your Emotional Awareness   Perhaps *the* essential way of knowing how your involvement in your children's sports affects them is going to be through your feelings. The more sensitive you are, the more accurately you will perceive what your children are feeling. If they are feeling pressure at a competition because of your presence, for example, you will recognize it a lot faster through your emotions than any other monitoring system you have. Emotional awareness is what gives you an insight and sensitivity into them that allows you to see below the surface, where the deeper truths are. The greater your emotional awareness becomes, the greater your perception, empathy, understanding, and compassion will be.

What if you have had little experience dealing with your emotions, and you do not relate to them very well? There is a choice then that you have to make. You can remain the same, or you can recognize that love itself is an emotion and to experience it to the fullest, you need to be willing to feel to the fullest. Are you willing to have the courage to begin the process of learning how to feel more deeply?

It is scary to open up to your emotions. You will have to be more vulnerable than you have ever been. You may have to give up your need to control others and allow their feelings into your life at a much more real level. You may find that you have had a different emotional effect upon your children—and others—than you thought you did. You may even have to risk finding out who the real you is.

Yet, with all these potential changes and risks, you will be embarking upon one of the most valuable processes you can do in a lifetime—for yourself and everyone you love. You will add dimensions to yourself and your relationships that you cannot even imagine at this point. And you will be giving a gift to your children that will add to their lives forever.

Children live and respond to their lives emotionally, not logically. It is your emotional awareness, more than any other aspect of you, that will help you see the real them.

Find Out How Your Children Feel about Your Being at Their Competitions
Asking your children how they feel about your being at their competitions seems like such an obvious thing to do, yet a high percentage of parents never seem to do it. Some have been genuinely surprised when I have asked them, "Have you talked to your son about how he feels when you come to his competitions?" It is as if that thought had never occurred to them.

When you do talk to your children, you know they will often tell you what they think you want to hear. They are afraid of hurting you, or of hurting themselves (by how you might react). With the issue of your coming to their competitions, you can make it safer for them to be honest. Tell them that, if they would feel more comfortable if you did not come to certain competitions, it is okay with you.

Often kids have asked their parents not to come to the big competitions— it made them too nervous—but they did want them to come to the less important ones. And then again, many kids have asked their parents not to come to certain competitions, only to discover that they missed their being there.

The key is to give your children choice. Most children enjoy having their parents around to support them. If your children do feel any discomfort with your being involved, your asking them how they feel about it gives them the opportunity to express their feelings. This then becomes the starting place for finding a solution everyone can live with.

Ask Your Spouse, or a Friend, What Messages You Give to Your Children When You Are at a Competition Sometimes you may genuinely be unaware of what messages you are giving to your children when you are at their competitions. But your spouse, or a friend, will usually know. Many parents, in their enthusiasm and concern, can put enormous pressure upon their children, but they do not see it. Talk with your spouse or a friend. Ask her or him what she or he sees. It can be invaluable feedback that will help you better support your children.

If your spouse or friend happens to tell you that you are negatively affecting your children, the real question then becomes this: Will you hear what he or she has to say—and will you act upon it?

All too often there are situations when a wife, for example, is very direct with her husband about how his dominating behavior is negatively affecting their children, but the husband ignores her—or agrees with her—and continues with the same behavior. The wife becomes very frustrated. The husband does not seem to care, or becomes frustrated with his "meddling" wife. And the children? Their feelings end up being ignored.

It takes courage to hear the truth, and it takes will and love to want to change. If you do happen to get feedback that indicates you need to change your attitude or behavior, are you willing to love your children enough to change? Your willingness to change, to even think about what your spouse or friend is telling you, is an issue of love. Your children need your love, but they do not know how to ask you to love them more. However, you can decide to do it *because* you love them.

If you get positive feedback from your spouse or friend, wonderful. This helps you know you are on the right path.

Are Your Needs Greater than Your Children's Needs? To see if your involvement in your children's sports might be creating pressure on them, ask yourself, "Is my need to be involved greater than my children's need to participate?" In other words, how important is it for you to be a part of what they do in their lives? Are you involved for the love and fun of it, so you can be there for them? Or is it a greater type of need? Are you living your life through their lives? Do you need them to give your life meaning?

Being involved in your children's activities, competitive sports in this case, because you want to be is one thing. But being involved because you *need* to be is an entirely different matter. Your life may have more meaning because you have children, but do you need children to have meaning in your life? Would you still have meaning in your life if you did not have your children's activities to be involved in?

If you need to be involved with them, they will feel it, and that need will put pressure on them. They cannot live their life for you. It is far too great a burden to place upon them. If they continually feel your need—a need they can never fill—they will probably end up resenting you for controlling their lives.

A high percentage of parents live their lives through their kids. They are deeply invested in everything their children do. Some would have little excitement in their lives if they did not have their children's lives to focus on.

Others focus on their children as a way to avoid dealing with the problems and frustrations in their marriages, or with their lives in general. These are the parents who can put the greatest pressure upon their children, often crushing their spirits before they reach their early teens. They are also usually the last ones to recognize what they are doing.

What are your needs? Are they greater than your children's needs? Are they balanced? It is a valuable question to ask yourself, especially when you are using it as a guideline to see if your behavior might be putting pressure upon your child.

If you suspect that you might have a need beyond what is natural for most parents but are unsure, ask what your spouse or a friend sees in your motivations. They will have a good idea of whether you seem to have a strong need or not.

Find Out How Your Children Act When You Are Not at a Competition—Compared to When You Are A very effective way to see if your children feel pressure when you are at one of their competitions is to ask their coach or a parent you are friendly with how your children act when you are not there.

If you find out that your children do act differently, talk to them. Ask them how they feel, and if they would rather you did not come. Most younger kids want their parents at competitions unless they feel a lot of pressure from them. Most older kids are more content being with their peers, though some want their parents there too.

If your children would rather you not come to their competitions or a particular event, ask them why. They may fear that you will be judgmental or feel disappointed in them if they do not do very well.

If you have acted that way in the past, their feelings are understandable. Then you need to look at why you reacted that way—and how you can change to make them feel more secure. If you have not acted that way, find out why they fear your judgment or disappointment. Just talking about it can often solve the problem for them, especially if you reassure them that you will not judge them or be disappointed in them personally.

After talking things over, if they still prefer that you do not come to their competitions, try skipping a few. See how they feel. See how you feel. If you are like most parents, you will understandably feel left out if you cannot come. But if you are willing to be flexible and show that your needs, though important, are not automatically more important than your children's needs, there is usually a way to work things out so everyone feels fulfilled.

Just your willingness to be sensitive to them and to examine your own actions will go a long way in changing their perception of you, making them feel more secure.

Interestingly enough, some parents have not gone to certain competitions in deference to their children's wishes, only to find out their kids ended up missing them—and asked them if they would come next time.

It Is Easier Not to Coach Your Children Many parents coach their children. It is natural to offer them guidance, particularly if you have an athletic background. You might even have experience in your child's sport. At the same time, it is always a risky proposition, for your very presence at an athletic competition can bring about a certain anxiety in your children.

If you add being their coach on top of being their parent, you are creating one more very significant source of potential pressure to their lives. It is far easier to let club coaches or other parents coach your children. They do not have a parent/child relationship—with all its expectations, complexities, and conflicts—with your children. They are not raising your children, nor are your children looking for their primary security from them. Club coaches may feel, and in fact be, very close to your children, but they will never have the same psychological connection that you have. This allows them the freedom to have a different perception, insight, and relationship. All of these conditions make it far easier for someone else to coach your children.

There is another problem in a parent coaching situation: It sets up a double set of pressures for your children. All children want their parents' approval, and all athletes want their coach's approval, especially when they are younger. As a coach, no matter how safe you try to make children feel, they will still want to please you and succeed for you—but now it is for you the parent *and* for you the coach.

Another question you might ask yourself is: If you do coach your children, is it possible to keep your expectations, hopes, angers, issues of control, and personal concerns about their safety and emotional status completely out of your mind?

After weighing everything, if you still decide you want to coach your children, start off by asking them how they feel about it. If it turns out they are not all right with it, it is much wiser to let someone else coach them. It is their sport and their life.

On the other hand, if they are okay with it, try it out and watch how it goes. Talk to them on a regular basis about how they feel. Look honestly at your own feelings. Does your coaching negatively affect your son or daughter in any way? Does it negatively affect you? If your coaching puts either one of you in a negative position, you need to make a significant change of some kind. Talk it over with them, to see if you can find a solution.

If you have a spouse, talk the situation over with him or her. Your spouse's perception is valuable and probably more accurate than your own.

If you do not really want to coach your children, but you just want to offer a "little help" from the sidelines, be careful how you do it. Helping out is one thing, but you should not need them to succeed. If you have too much of an investment in how well they do, they will feel it. It will come across in the way you help them, through your expressions, your tone of voice, your body language, your eyes, and other things you do. Your "need" for their success will ultimately compromise whatever help you might offer.

There are many parents who do offer advice, without needing their children to succeed. They just want to help. This approach can work, and it can be fun for both parent and child.

The question "How can I be involved in my children's sport without putting unwanted pressure on them?" is a complex one that speaks to the very heart of this book. The answer deserves depth and consideration. Certainly what has been offered here is not the entire answer. It is, in many ways, only the beginning of an answer. It is your willingness to learn and the quality of your experience and knowledge that you garner along the way that will ultimately help you answer it. And it is your love for your children that will guide you.

Question 5—"My son/daughter does not seem to be fully committed or motivated in his or her sport. I know he/she is holding back. Why is this, and how can I help him/her?"

Some athletes seem driven, while others clearly are not. Some focus on nothing but their goals. Others will not even set goals, or if they do, they will not follow through. What causes these differences?

This might seem like a simple question with a simple answer, yet it is anything but. If you reflect upon what you have read so far, you will see not only the tremendous emotional complexity of your children, but also how your behavior plays into the development of their thought and feeling patterns, as well as the very formation of their personality. It is not that you entirely form your children. You do not. They have their own talents and strengths and their own minds. But there are specific things that do affect their motivation.

The interplay between their birth order, personality types, relationship with you, and beliefs about their value and worth all influence their motivations and level of commitment. You can also add to the mix their fears, hurts, angers, and other unresolved emotions, not to mention their relationships with friends and siblings. And even all of these things do not cover the full complexity of your children's motivations. Keeping this in mind, let us take a look at how to answer the question.

There are some very specific reasons why some children and adolescents are less committed, and thus less motivated, than others. Some of these are obvious—fear of failure, fear of success, sibling pressures, fear of disappointing you. While many parents understand the emotional side of these reasons, others see only through their intellect—without an emotional awareness of what their children are feeling. These parents do not fully relate to the pressures and fears their children are experiencing. They often put pressure on them to straighten up and do a better job, which only increases their children's concerns and often causes them to hold back even more.

The way to approach the problem of a lack of commitment and motivation with young athletes is to love them enough not to judge them, to try to understand what they are feeling. Try to go below the surface. They have their reasons for backing away from commitment and motivation. Granted, some will be laziness, avoidance of responsibility, or rebellion of one sort or another; but most of their reasons are going to be about the emotions of fear, pain, and love.

The more you understand your children's emotional reasons for holding back in their sport, the more you can help them.

Fear of Commitment

You would be amazed how many children, and adolescents particularly, are afraid to totally commit to their sports. In numerous seminars with young athletes I have asked the question, "How many of you know that, to some degree, you are holding yourselves back from giving it everything you've got?" In every situation, a significant number of the athletes in the room—as many as three out of four—have raised their hand.

When asked why they were afraid to totally commit and give it everything they had, most said they had never really thought about why they were holding back. They just knew they were. They felt it. And many would never have admitted it openly until they looked around and noticed others raising their hands. Then they, somewhat sheepishly, raised theirs too.

There are many different reasons why young athletes hold back, but there is one reason that is common to them all. No matter what their sport or where they live, they always bring up this reason. If they fully commit, they might find out they do not have what it takes to succeed. That thought is so scary to them that many have trouble even expressing it. Some begin to cry just at the thought of it.

This is what so many are really afraid of: If they do not have the talent, if they do not have what it takes, they will be looked down upon, judged, rejected, and humiliated. If they give it their all and fail, their fear is that they are not good enough to be loved. They are afraid of not being accepted, of not belonging, of feeling separated from others. They do not usually phrase their responses with the word love, but that is what their underlying fear is all about. They are afraid if they go all out and fail, they are not good enough to be loved, which is why so many hold back. They are too afraid of taking that risk.

Though some young people, particularly adolescents, will not commit to anything, competitive athletes are usually willing to take on more responsibility. Just by participating in a sport they have to have a certain amount of commitment—to train, to be part of a team, and to compete. If your children are holding back, it is probably for reasons other than laziness, rebellion, or just plain irresponsibility.

Here are some suggestions you might try to help your children with their fears about commitment:

❑ Though a lot of young people feel uncomfortable talking about their emotions, it is always wise and loving to give them the opportunity to open up. Talk to your children about commitment. Find out what they think it means. Ask them what they are afraid is going to happen if they totally commit to their sport. Try to get them to talk about their feelings. That is always the first place to start—with feelings.

❑ Reassure them that you love them, that you always will, whether they fully commit to their sport or not. Talk to them about how learning to have the courage to commit to anything is an invaluable part of growing up. And let them know that whenever they are committed to anything, sports or otherwise, you will not judge them if they fail. Rather, you will feel proud of them for their willingness to put themselves on the line.

❑ Talk to them about the consequences of holding back in life. Without judging them for holding back, help them understand what happens when someone is not willing to risk. Explain how they can never really find out who they are or what they are capable of achieving, without fully committing to something and risking.

❑ Help your children see that fear of commitment—for whatever reason—is a normal reaction for anyone to have, particularly young people. Talk about the times in your life when you held back on fully committing to something.

❑ Talk about the real value of commitment—it allows the opportunity to reach into ourselves and discover our inner strengths and talents, our hidden treasures, and ultimately, who we are.

❑ Share the times in your life when you have been fully committed to something and how it helped you discover your sense of power, as well as other aspects of yourself you could never have experienced without being fully committed.

❑ Talk about how learning to commit to something, a competitive sport in this case, is an important and valuable step in a young person's process of taking responsibility for their lives.

❑ Do not lose sight of the fact that your children usually have emotional reasons for backing away from full commitment. In some cases they just do not want the responsibility, and you may have to set reasonable boundaries to help them finish what they started out to do. But in so many other cases, especially with young athletes, it is fear that prevents them from fully committing.

Look for what they are afraid of, exercising understanding and patience. Help them find and talk about their fears. Even if they are unwilling to talk about their emotions, if you understand their fears, you can be there for them, ready to talk if they ever need you. Empathy goes a long way. This can strengthen your relationship and make it easier for them to take the next step toward being more fully committed.

In time and with your support and understanding, your children can learn that commitment to a competitive sport, or anything else, can teach them more about themselves than they could ever have imagined.

The Fear of Failure—and Success

With a society so focused on success and performance, with star athletes collecting so much money, with hero worship raising athletes' popularity to international status, and with young athletes linking their value to their performance, failure and success have a lot of inflated and distorted energy around them.

Young athletes are well aware of how others treat them when they fail. They face potential judgement and humiliation, often from their own parents as well as from coaches and teammates. Failure can cause painful feelings of disappointment, hurt, and—for many athletes who fail consistently—a sense of despair and shame.

Many athletes try to protect themselves from having to face this potential pain by refusing to commit themselves fully. With less investment, there is less risk of failure, disappointment, and pain.

Then there is the fear of success, which is far more frightening than dealing with potential failure. Successful athletes are continually expected to live up to that success. They have demonstrated a certain level of expertise, and the natural assumption by most coaches, teammates, parents, and the general public is that they will continue succeeding. When everyone expects an athlete to win, or to at least continue being successful, it automatically puts a heavier burden on that athlete to perform.

Successful athletes have far more to lose than average athletes. There is reputation, image, and often charisma that go along with success. There is also admiration and respect from coaches, teammates, competitors, family, and the general public. All of these things are potentially at stake if an athlete does not continue being successful. And a significant failure for a star athlete carries great pain, potential judgment, and humiliation. That failure can be national in scope if it happens during a national championship and international in scope if it happens during an Olympics or a world championship.

There are other problems many successful athletes face. If they are involved in a team sport, sometimes other athletes on the team are jealous. They can ignore and reject the star who showed them up. And less-committed athletes, who like to take it easy in training sessions and often fool around to further avoid the training, do not like a go-getter, the one who works harder than them. These less-committed athletes can be very hurtful, using judgment and cutting remarks as a way to punish the committed ones for exposing them.

Fear of failure or success is something all young athletes face. They cannot escape it. It is not bad or unnatural for them to experience these fears. The more you can understand the nature of their fears, the easier it will be for you to help them.

It takes courage to be a young competitive athlete. There is no guarantee of success or failure, only of an opportunity to try. You, your love, and your understanding are their support system. You can help them through the rough spots by talking and listening to them and by being there when they need you.

When it comes to facing fear, you are the one your son or daughter needs the most.

Emotional Turmoil Can Affect Motivation

Another significant reason why some young athletes are not fully committed can be emotional turmoil. Divorce, parental fighting, sibling problems, a death in the family, alcoholism, troubles with friends, financial problems, or any other like situation usually will cause emotional confusion and a sense of isolation in young people.

These conditions can make it very difficult for those who are participating in competitive athletics to maintain their focus. It often appears that they lack motivation. In fact, they do; they are focused on their turmoil, not their sport.

Children and adolescents try to deal with their confusion and sense of isolation by attempting to suppress or deny whatever they are feeling. They do not know any other way to deal with their emotions. The problem here is that the types of emotions that young people feel when they are faced with significant problems—anger, hurt, fear, pain, humiliation, issues of betrayal and abandonment— cannot be suppressed without consequences.

It takes effort, will, and energy to suppress emotions, particularly painful ones. This creates a constant physical, mental, and emotional energy drain, which in turn causes an imbalance in one's life. This will manifest in unexpected failures or extreme reactions to the normal pressures that young athletes continually face. They may become susceptible to emotional breakdowns, irrational behavior, and in many cases, physical injury as a way of crying out for help. There are a number of young—and older—athletes who finally crack under the weight of their pent-up, emotional dams. It happens all the time.

In the seminars I lead, where athletes are given the opportunity and security to talk about feelings they have been suppressing, their emotions just spill out of them. Some are as young as ten years of age. Others have held on until they were in their twenties. All of these young people have talked about losing focus and motivation because of their inability to deal with the emotional turmoil they were experiencing in their lives.

It is worth noting that not all athletes are affected by emotional pain in the same way. Some can rise above it, though not forever. And not all athletes lose their motivation or commitment to their sports because of the turmoil they may be experiencing. Yet, emotional turmoil still remains a major cause of motivation loss in young athlete's lives. It is always worth looking into if you sense it is there.

Young athletes often hold back. This does not mean they will always do this, nor does it necessarily mean anything is wrong with them or with you as a parent. What is important is that you try to understand them and refrain from being judgmental. So many parents judge their kids—and hurt them by doing so—for not committing more to their sport, or not excelling more. Many never look beneath the surface for the deeper answers as to why they might be doing that.

Your children are trying to find their way through life, and often they feel frightened—of not fitting in, of not measuring up, of not being liked, of ultimately not being good enough to be loved. Commitment, with all its risks, can easily increase their fear.

Sometimes they need a nudge this way or that. Sometimes they need strict boundaries. And sometimes they just need time. With your help, patience, and understanding, they will have an easier time making it.

Siblings Who Hold Back

Some families have more than one child in competitive sports. Often they are in the same sport, like swimming and soccer. It is quite common that issues come up between siblings. There is usually a natural competition between them, though many are friends and supporters, rather than competitors.

One of the most difficult situations facing siblings is when they are same sex in the same sport. It is common to see younger siblings (much more with sisters than with brothers), particularly from eleven to fifteen, feel afraid to surpass their older siblings for fear of hurting them. Many have told me they are consciously holding themselves back from improving so that they will not become better than their older sibling.

The problem they face is that they have always looked up to their older siblings—often idolizing them. Usually, they are in the same sport specifically because their older siblings are in it. It is difficult for them to suddenly be the better one. That has always been the older one's position. They know it signals a change in their relationship, and it can cause great stress and turmoil in them—which causes difficulty with their motivation.

When these situations come up in seminars, it is always important to give the older siblings the opportunity to express how they feel about their younger siblings surpassing them. Usually they say they do feel hurt, frustrated, or jealous of their abilities. They are used to being the better one, the one who sets the example, the leader, the one who does everything first—because they are older. It is difficult and often painful for them to suddenly change places with their younger sister or brother. Being the better athlete is part of their identity. Becoming the second-ranked athlete can make them feel as if they are failures.

Yet, despite these feelings, of all the older siblings who have spoken up, none of them has ever wanted their younger siblings to hold themselves back. And they always tell them that, right there in the seminar, usually with tears and a lot of emotion.

Another difficult situation that comes up with siblings of the same sex in the same sport is when the younger ones are continually compared to the older ones by their parents in a negative light. They are constantly reminded that they are not measuring up to the older brother or sister. Statements such as, "Your brother was already one of the best athletes on the team when he was your age" and "If you would just try a little harder you could be as good as your sister" are common. This type of treatment will lead to, at the very least, resentment toward the parents. It can also affect the younger sibling's commitment and motivation. Many hold themselves back, feeling that it is simply too much pressure to always have to measure up.

Then there are those younger siblings who excel and surpass their older siblings, but it often sets up a pattern in which they feel they always have to compete with that sibling for their parents' love. It can easily compromise the relationship between the two siblings for many years—or a lifetime.

In addition, there are younger siblings who hold themselves back simply to get their parents' attention. Countless parents ask the question, "What is the problem with my son? He doesn't seem motivated." When I ask them if they are paying a lot of attention to the boy, helping him, worrying about him, they always answer yes. It is a common and very effective way for younger kids to get attention. Most often their motivation is based on their resentment toward their parents for giving their older sibling, who they resent also, more attention than them.

There is one more aspect of siblings who hold back. Some older siblings hold themselves back so their younger brothers or sisters will not have too much to live up to. They know their parents are constantly comparing the younger ones to them, and they know how much it is hurting them. Many siblings—older and younger—have told their parents they did not like the comparisons, and though some parents changed their behavior, many either denied their actions or acknowledged what they were doing while continuing to make the comparisons.

I will never forget the seminar in which one of the better athletes in the country surprised everyone in the room by talking about how he had held himself back for years to protect his younger brother from his parents' constant comparisons and judgment. The younger brother was not only shocked at hearing this, but so moved by his older brother's desire to protect him that he burst out crying and was unable to stop for several minutes.

What can work well to help ease and heal the situation between younger siblings who are surpassing their older brothers or sisters, or older siblings who are holding back, is to have them talk to each other about how important they are to one another. When these situations with siblings come up in seminars, I ask them if they have ever spoken about how much they love each other. Normally, on their own, they do not talk about the love they feel—especially boys. Yet, when asked to express their feelings toward each other in the seminar, they have always professed their love for each other in such a beautiful, tearful, and meaningful way that it has touched every other athlete in the room.

This kind of caring interaction usually frees up the younger siblings to let themselves achieve to their highest potential. And the older ones learn they are not failures simply because their younger siblings happen to be more talented or skilled than they are. They both realize how important they are to each other, and that helps them rise above their fears and move forward.

The older children who are protecting their younger siblings need the help of their parents—you—to stop the comparisons. Then they can be free. Generally, parents know they are comparing their kids, but most do not see the negative emotional impact it is having upon them. Many times, one parent does see what is happening and repeatedly tells the other parent to stop because it is hurting both siblings. Sadly, the other parent all too often is more interested in results rather than feelings, believing that comparisons are a good way to motivate children. They are not; comparisons only hurt them.

Even if a sibling did compete based on a parent's comparisons, it would only be out of fear of being hurt by further comparisons. What that parent is really saying is, "In my eyes you are not as good and lovable as your older sibling because you don't achieve as much."

If you recognize that you are comparing your children to each other, consider the damage you can do and the pain you can cause your children. Consider that your comparisons can set up lifetime patterns of unhealthy behavior for them. And consider the shame you are passing on to them. And then change.

It is very effective to simply sit down and meet with those you are comparing and tell them what you recognize and that you want to change—and apologize. Give them the opportunity to talk about their frustrations, anger, hurt, and whatever else they might be feeling. This can be the healing that is needed.

Helping Your Children Deal with Their Emotions

The previous section looked at different ways to help your children deal with their fear of commitment. Let us take it further and look at other emotions, in addition to fear. Whenever you see a lack of motivation, trying to find out what your children are feeling is a good first step to helping them.

Emotional ups and downs are a part of life for young people, whether they center on fear or any other emotion. In large part, this is because they are too young too know how to respond to what they are feeling. Suppression and denial are normal ways of dealing with uncomfortable feelings.

Anything you can do to help them learn how to feel their emotions rather than avoid them will be very healthy for them. It is important to understand that children and adolescents will rarely fully respond to all their feelings. They cannot; they are too young to have the emotional capacity to do that. But your willingness to talk about feelings—yours and theirs—and to help them open up, to whatever extent they are willing, can make it easier for them to begin learning about their emotions.

Another important thing to know is that there may be some particularly painful things that will occur in your children's lives that they will have real difficulty responding to until they are older. It can simply be too much pain for them to face at a young age. They usually avoid facing it by denying it. In these situations, children and teens will generally not want to talk about whatever pain they are experiencing—that would make them have to face it. So if you get the silent treatment over some issues, it may be because they are not yet ready to open up to feeling that pain again.

With adolescents in particular—boys especially—you may get the silent treatment over all emotional issues. This is because adolescents are far more frightened of their emotions than children are. They are experiencing psychological, physiological, emotional, and hormonal changes all at the same time. They are also separating from you, trying to find their own identities. All these changes happening at the same time make uncomfortable or painful emotions even more scary for them to face. Yet, though they may be uncommunicative, do not give up on them. In an appropriate way, keep offering to listen or to talk if they ever feel the need. That will be very reassuring to them, although most would have difficulty admitting to it. It might sound too much like they need you. Well, the fact is, they do—very much.

One of the most effective ways to help young people learn about their emotions is to encourage them to express their feelings, especially when they are younger. This way you are continually giving them the message that it is natural to express feelings—and that you value their feelings. At appropriate times, when your children are feeling hurt, angry, fearful, or any other such emotions, but they are not sharing those feelings with you or they look like they are stuck, help them out. Ask them how they are feeling. Give them a chance to respond. If they do open up to you, try listening without giving advice. Just being heard is very important to them. After they have expressed themselves, if it seems that they need some advice or you know that they want your advice, ask them if they would like to hear your thoughts on the situation.

When asked about their feelings, many adolescents will say "I'm fine" or make some other such denial. If they do, be patient. Sometimes they need the space to be alone with their feelings before they can talk about them. Other times, they may want to talk but do not know how or where to begin. In your way, always let them know you are there, ready and willing to listen to them. The more you talk about your own feelings—in a responsible and vulnerable way—the easier you make it for them to express theirs.

Another effective way for your children to get in touch with and feel, and let go of, their emotions is to write about what they are feeling—to do "journaling," as outlined in Chapter 10. They can write about anything, any emotion, whatever they are feeling. Journaling allows them the freedom to express themselves in their own words and in private. It is easy for young people to do, extremely beneficial, and it affords them an opportunity to learn how to respond to their feelings.

Suggest this to your children. Get them a spiral notebook. They may not follow through, but at least they will have the opportunity whenever they feel the need.

What is important here is that they feel what they are expressing, whether they are talking with you or writing in their notebook. The process of releasing—and healing—a hurt, an anger, a fear, or any other emotion happens by feeling that emotion. The more they can feel their emotions, the more they can let go of them.

Question 6—Sometimes I feel like I want my children to succeed a little too much, which puts pressure on them. How can I want them to succeed without putting any pressure on them?

This question goes right to the heart of so many parent-child relationships in youth sports. A part of every child's natural drive is to succeed, whether as a young athlete or something else. Their quest for success is one of the most significant ways in which they learn about themselves. And you want your children to do well and be successful. It is fun, full of adventure, and rewarding for all concerned. So how do you go about wanting them to be successful without inadvertently putting any extra pressure on them?

Perhaps the best way of knowing what to do is to start by asking yourself if you need your children to succeed. How much of a personal investment in their success do you have? This question may sound similar to an earlier question that also addressed need, but that need concerned being physically involved in your children's sports. This type of need has to do with their specific level of success.

Do You Need Your Children to Succeed?

Normally, most parents I meet deny—usually immediately—that they need their children to succeed. It often is an assumption, rather than something they really take the time to look at. It is uncomfortable to see themselves in that light, and some can be truly unaware of how strong their need is.

At the same time, it is normal for any parent to need, to some extent, their children to succeed. It can be considered a form of feedback that they are doing a good job at parenting, though it is more valid if their children are succeeding more for themselves than for their parents. There is always a natural tendency for children to want to succeed for their parents, as their way of loving them. There is nothing wrong with this. But it should be a healthy balance, not a situation where parents' needs are far greater than their children's.

As you evaluate your own parenting, the more you recognize whatever needs you may have in regard to your children's success, the easier it is to balance and change them if necessary. This is an essential and ongoing process in any relationship of love, especially with children because they are so vulnerable.

The simple truth that most of us know is that no one can fill our needs for us. We have to learn to do that ourselves. It is part of the maturing process. Children, on the other hand, cannot fill their own needs. They need their parents, teachers, and coaches along the way to help them learn how to do it. That is why the development of the Whole Self is so important. It will give them a broad foundation to stand on so they can become more capable of responding to their own needs in life.

So how do you recognize if you need—and how much you need—your children to succeed?

What follows are two lists. One consists of more obvious actions, the kind you often see demonstrated in public. The other list is made up of questions to consider. Both are designed to help you look at your level of need. The key here is not to assume you know your needs—even if you think you do. Explore and reflect, discovering what you may.

Here are several actions that parents with a strong need for their children's success demonstrate:

- ❏ Yelling in disapproval at children when they fail to meet the parents' expectations of performance
- ❏ Being critical or condescending after a poor performance by a child
- ❏ Humiliating a child after he/she has failed in a competition
- ❏ Making winning and losing far too important

❑ Having little patience when a child is in a slump, or when he or she is not improving fast enough
❑ Telling children that winning is what is most important in sports
❑ Responding positively only after "acceptable" performances
❑ Constantly comparing a child to a better-performing sibling
❑ Constantly comparing in a critical way a child's unsuccessful performances to what other more successful athletes are achieving
❑ Always focusing on what a child does wrong
❑ Focusing far more on the "successful child" than on other children in the family
❑ Continually switching to new coaches—trying to find the one who will make the child successful

This list is pretty straightforward. A significant percentage of parents in all the different competitive sports act in most or all of these ways. A significant percentage do not. You may do some or none of these things. You may even be appalled by what you see some parents do to their kids—it can anger you. At the same time, you yourself still might have some need for your child to succeed, but you may be more subtle in how you act it out.

Usually it is obvious when you are critical, disapproving, or do something that causes intimidation or fear in your children, particularly when it comes to their failure to live up to your expectations. But what could you be saying and doing that is more subtle unintentionally or unconsciously? Are you exhibiting behavior that may also create a sense of intimidation, insecurity, or fear?

Here is an example of a mother who was not critical or outwardly judgmental in any particular way, but who did other things that were just as damaging, though she was unaware of it:

A father told me about his wife's relationship with their son before we began the athlete's seminar. He wanted me to try and help the boy; he sensed his son was feeling a lot of pressure but could never get him to talk about it.

He began by telling me that the mother was very involved in everything their son did. She loved him very much, so much so, she told him, that she would make sure he had every opportunity that she herself never had. And she did. He participated in several activities in school and various sports. It turned out he was talented. He did well.

She continually told him that he was a great talent—he could do anything and everything. She came to all his competitions and school activities and became his strongest supporter.

The boy was good at what he participated in, no doubt, even though he was only eleven years old. But the father felt he was having real trouble with his mother's constant hovering and telling him how good he was. He talked to his wife about his feelings, but she did not agree. Everything was fine according to her.

With this information, along with the coach telling me that he too sensed the boy was feeling a lot of pressure, I wanted to meet this boy.

I saw him on the outskirts of the group when we began the seminar. The coach made sure I knew where he was, hoping I would find a way to talk to him. All during the seminar I tried to find a way, even once directly asking him if he wanted to talk about anything. He did not.

After the second day had ended, I had the opportunity to see the boy alone. I asked if we could take a walk. He agreed.

"I understand you are a pretty good athlete—in many sports," I began.

"Yeah . . . I guess so," he said.

"How does it feel to be so gifted?" I said.

He went silent. The word *gifted* seemed to get to him.

"You know," I continued, "being gifted can be a double-edged sword. You can do many things well, but then a lot of people have high expectations for you, which you sometimes can feel you have to live up to. That can be tough."

We were sitting on a bench. He turned his head to the side, away from me, and said nothing for a minute or so. Though he tried, he could not stop the tears from running down his face. He wiped his eyes as casually as he could and then tried to turn all the way around so his body was facing away from me, but there was not enough room on the bench to do that, so he finally gave up and just sat with his head down, crying softly.

I put a gentle arm around his shoulders and said, "It feels a lot better to just cry when you feel it coming up." We sat there for several minutes, while he cried and cried. When he finally stopped, I said, "Why don't you tell me about it?"

"This year has been really hard," he began. "My mother came to everything I did. Every time I did well she told me how great I was going to be—that I was going to be the best in everything. How can I do that—in everything? She wants me to be the best in everything! I'll never be able to do it. I don't even want to try anymore; it's too hard. But how can I can quit? What will she think of me then?" He began crying all over again, bigger tears this time.

While I waited, I thought of what the father had told me, how he had told the mother how much pressure their son was feeling, how the mother did not believe it, saying the boy was fine.

The boy continued. "Every night, my mother asks me, how did practice go, what did you do in school? Then she wants to know every single thing I did—in detail," he said. "We can't just have dinner and talk about something else. It's always about me—and how good I'm going to be."

He became silent. I waited again. Then, he shocked me. "I think it's just better to stop trying in everything—sports, school, everything—that way there will be

no more pressure and no more expectations—and I won't disappoint my mother
. . . . The best way out is to kill myself. And I know how to do it."

It had just slipped out of his mouth, spoken softly, evenly, without emotion. I
nearly missed the words. I waited for a while, then spoke.

"Well . . . you could do that if you wanted," I said. "But a lot of people would
miss you, including your parents, your friends, your coach, and your teammates.
In fact, I'll bet if your mom knew how you felt, she would be very sad and sorry
for making you feel this way. I'll bet she would change, a lot, and you would not
have to do anything you did not want to do, and she would love you even more
for helping her understand your needs.

"You know, sometimes parents can't always see how they affect their children.
But given the opportunity, they can change."

He sat quietly, saying nothing.

After a while, I added, "How do you think she would feel if you never gave her
the chance to understand you and change? I can help you talk to her if you like
. . . . Would you like my help?"

He still had not said anything. Then, I caught a barely perceptible nod.

"Is that a yes?"

"Yes . . . " he said.

We went to his house and I told his mother I wanted to talk to her. I laid
everything out, telling her about our conversation, about the pressure he was
feeling, his despair, and finally about his talking about suicide.

She turned pale, nearly white, and collapsed against a table. She was silent for
several minutes, tears in her eyes.

His mother then talked of how she had tried so much to be a good mother,
giving her son everything that she never had. She spoke of the anger and hurt
she still felt toward her parents over the opportunities they denied her when she
was growing up, how much that hurt had created a deep need to provide her
son with every opportunity possible—and how that need had blinded her to
what her son had been feeling. And that she did not really want to believe her
husband when he continually pointed it out.

That day she and her son went for a long walk. She told him how sorry she
was for putting so much pressure on him. She talked about her childhood and
teen years, explaining her motivations, and then she apologized again. She told
him that if he wanted to play sports and do school activities or if he wanted to
quit, it was okay. She would always love him no matter what he did in his life.

I spoke to the father some time later to see how things were going. He said
the mother had kept her word. She did change and so did the boy. There were
still conflicts between mother and son, but they were getting along better than
they had in a long time.

Your words, or lack of them, the things you talk about, your looks, tones of
voices, moods, and questions can have as great an effect upon a child as more

obvious forms of behavior. Your need may not even be very strong; but if it is there, your children will sense it. The subtleties are the difficult things to be aware of.

How do you go about discovering your less-obvious forms of behavior that give your children the message that you need them to succeed? Here are several questions for you to consider. If you take your time, considering everything that each question implies, both in thought and feeling, you can discover a wealth of information about yourself. For example, the first question is, "How do you react when your child fails?" Look at everything about this question you can think of.

❑ How do you feel about their failure?
❑ Do you know what the look on your face is right after they have failed?
❑ What do you say to your son or daughter after a failure?
❑ How do you handle your own disappointment?
❑ Do you automatically tell your boy or girl what he or she did wrong, trying to help them?
❑ Do you try to make them feel better by saying nothing?
❑ Do you blame the coach?

Look below the surface when you answer each question. Do not be tempted to give an immediate, automatic reaction, such as "I don't think I do that" or "Well, maybe I react a little." Be willing to ask yourself, "How does my little reaction affect my child?" Take the time to reflect upon your answers—for several minutes if necessary. You might even come back to the same question and look at it again the next day to reflect further.

These questions are meant to help you look more closely at your relationship with your children, so that you can see with greater perception what your emotional impact upon them is. It is always helpful to keep in mind that it can be difficult to acknowledge your behavior if you feel uncomfortable, hurt, shameful, or embarrassed, if you recognize you might be hurting or negatively affecting others, especially your children. Yet none of these feelings, as uncomfortable as they may be, need to be your reason for acting without responsibility.

If you really want to cover all the bases when you look at these questions, ask your spouse, child, or a friend you trust to offer their observations. You might even read the questions together, you reflecting and then answering, then the other person offering how they see you. Whoever you ask might be able to see some things more clearly than you do.

If you discover that indeed you are demanding or intimidating at times—or even all the time—and you are having a negative impact upon your child, acknowledge yourself for having the courage to tell the truth. Know that now—because you know the truth—you can change.

Here is the second list of questions. It is not meant to be a complete list, but it will get you started. Keep searching for more of your own questions to ask. It is a very effective way to learn about yourself.

- ❑ How do you react when your kids fail?
- ❑ How important is it to you that they succeed?
- ❑ Do you need them to succeed?
- ❑ Do you judge yourself as a poor parent if they fail, that somehow you are not doing enough?
- ❑ Do you put a bumper sticker on your car that advertises your child as being the student of the week at his or her school?
- ❑ Do you follow a pro, college, or high school team, whose wins and losses significantly influence your emotions?
- ❑ Do you openly criticize athletes because they do not measure up to your standards?
- ❑ Do you continually remind your child that he or she is not living up to his or her potential?
- ❑ Do you always check up on your child to make sure he or she is training hard enough?
- ❑ Are you demanding of yourself about your need to excel and succeed?
- ❑ Are you a perfectionist?
- ❑ Are you highly competitive?
- ❑ Do you pay more attention to the more successful son or daughter than to the less successful one?
- ❑ Are you more interested in the college you want your child to go to or the college he or she wants to go to?
- ❑ Do you focus on your child's shortcomings and on what he or she lacks?
- ❑ Do you offer rewards, like money, for high achievements?
- ❑ Do you honestly believe doing your best is good enough, even if your children are mediocre in their performances?
- ❑ Do you talk a lot about your child's achievements to other family members, to other people, to your child?
- ❑ Do you make it known that it would help financially if your child earned a scholarship?
- ❑ Do you remind your child of the opportunities he or she has that you did not have?
- ❑ Do you frequently talk about how much money it is costing for your child to participate in his or her sport?
- ❑ Are you always correcting your child in such a way as to make him or her feel like he or she can never be good enough?
- ❑ Do you ever talk about how much time your child's sport takes away from your life?

As a rule of thumb, it is worth remembering that whatever significance you put on success in sports, and life in general, will always be communicated to your children. You cannot hide your true feelings or beliefs from them. This can be a positive or a negative, depending upon how you view success and failure.

If you have your own self-esteem tied up in succeeding, you will assuredly raise children to think and feel likewise—and you will put enormous pressure on them along the way. If you want your children to do well, and your own worth and value is not tied up in your—or your children's—success, you will make it much more secure for them to fail—and much easier for them to succeed.

You may not always know, or be aware of, your emotional impact upon your children, but you can always try to make it as loving as possible, whether they succeed or fail. And even if you make mistakes and say the wrong thing from time to time, your children will always know you love them if they see you care enough to continually examine yourself and change when appropriate—for them.

Every parent can find themselves out of balance with their needs sometimes, putting pressure on their children without even knowing it. The key is not to always strive to be perfectly in balance with your needs, but rather to try to correct imbalances when you see them.

Patience, Love, and Understanding

These three things are all you need and your children will not feel unduly pressured by your desire for their success. Sounds simple, right? Much of this book is about being able to do these three simple things—because they are not so simple.

The only way you can do these things—have patience, be loving, and understand your children—is to be emotionally grounded. That means you are aware of what you are feeling, so you can be sensitive to what your children are feeling. It also means you use your awareness to pay attention to your emotional impact on them, changing and being flexible when appropriate. And it means being willing to continually learn about yourself, so that you can sharpen and increase your awareness.

If you are willing to do these things—and you do not have to do them perfectly—you can develop patience, increase the depth of your love, and deepen your understanding of your children. So what is the key to doing these things so your children will not feel any extra pressure from you when you care about, support, and root for them in their games and competitions?

You could say, in one way or another, this entire book is about how you become more patient, loving, and understanding. And to a large degree, you would be right. As you have read, it is a complex process to learn, to deepen your awareness about your emotional self. It also takes time, desire, and perhaps most important, following through. So rather than repeat what has already been said, perhaps the best way to approach this is to look at the difficulties you might encounter, that would prevent you from achieving the patience, love, and understanding you seek.

The first difficulty you might face is making assumptions about how patient, loving, and understanding you think you already are, without really looking at yourself closely. What you think may be accurate; then again, it might not be. But you will not see that if you use only assumptions to guide you.

The second potential difficulty lies in whether you are willing to be vulnerable enough to feel your emotions on a deeper level than you do right now. This is the only way to increase your awareness. You have to go beyond your current emotional boundaries to learn more about your emotional self. This is true for all of us, no matter whether we feel deeply or not much at all, whether we have spent years working with our emotions or if we have never explored them.

This second potential problem can be the real stumbling block because of the way we are generally taught to avoid our feelings, or at least not to feel them too deeply. The way you feel and respond emotionally to your relationships and day-to-day life has become habitual unless you have consciously explored, worked with, and learned new habits. This does not happen just by growing older. It happens only by conscious choice and action.

My personal experience, in my own continuing growth and in working with others, has shown me how easy it is to become complacent about our emotions. We cannot assume if we ever truly want to grow.

You can learn about your emotions for the rest of your life and still not know yourself fully. There is an unending depth of awareness waiting for you to discover. It is your choice as to how far you go in your own journey of personal awareness. Your desire for expanding your capacity to be patient, loving, and understanding for your children can be your inspiration to go beyond where you currently are—and then go beyond again and again.

Use whatever parts of this book that you think are helpful to guide you. Talk to your spouse and friends, asking them for insight. Talk to your children. Tell them you do not want to put any pressure on them. Ask them how they would like to be supported by you. Through it all, you *can* find a way to support and root for your children without putting any pressure on them.

Question 7—My children often tell me I don't listen to them— that I don't hear them. How can I be a better listener?

Communication between parent and child is not always easy. At the very least, it takes patience, time, focus, desire, and particularly an emotional awareness. Listening, which is as much an art as a skill, is the key to any real communication and the bridge to understanding your children. Listening with all your senses—including that unseen and inexplicable part of you that goes beyond what you physically hear—will allow your ability to perceive what your children are saying to be that much more acute.

Listening with Your Intuitive Senses

Listening is quite magical if you think about it for a minute. So much of real listening is done with your intuitive senses. How many times have you sensed a son or daughter crying out in pain, yet he or she never uttered a word? How often have you sensed an emotional constriction—pain, anger, hurt, fear—in another, but that person never told you about it? When was the last time you knew a person was depressed, but they had not even recognized it themselves?

When you listen, you usually call upon your wisdom and intelligence to help you interpret what you are hearing. Yet, if you are not tuned in intuitively, you can easily miss hearing what your children might be trying to tell you. Children, especially ones in competitive sports who may be feeling pressures even they are not aware of, so often need help just in recognizing—let alone working through—what they are feeling. Your intuitive senses allow you to go beyond the logic of words and feel the depth and substance that lie beneath those words.

What is the key to sharpening your intuitive senses? Deepening your emotional awareness will increase your ability to sense unspoken requests. It is like throwing out a "sensitivity net" that scans what your children are feeling. All of your emotions, working in synergy with each other, form the net. The more deeply you feel, the more sensitive you will become, and the wider your net will be.

An insensitive person is one who does not feel very deeply. Their net is nonexistent, or it is very narrow and has holes in it. They cannot accurately pick up what their children, and others, are feeling.

Looking at it another way, emotionally numb parents can put enormous pressure upon their young athletes to win, yet they cannot see that their children are breaking under the weight of their expectations. They may notice something is off with their children, but they have difficulty understanding why. They typically explain it away to training, fatigue, or pre-competition jitters, but they rarely "sense" what their children are feeling and experiencing. They are too emotionally closed down.

When you attend competitions in youth sports and are standing on the sidelines or sitting in the stands, watch how certain parents relate to their children. You will see which ones are insensitive and reactive, though they rarely see it.

How many times have you wondered, "Doesn't that father see what he is doing to his son?" The answer is no, that father does not really see how he is affecting his son. He is not sensitive enough to hear *or* see what he is doing to him. Parents who cannot sense accurately block their ability to perceive truth that may be painfully obvious to everyone else. They cannot hear what their children are saying—or cannot say.

Children of these types of parents end up feeling invisible in their own homes. Few of their parents are aware of their inability to truly hear their children, nor do they see their devastating impact.

No matter where you may happen to be in your listening abilities, one of the best ways to enhance the art and skill of listening to your children—to be able to better understand and love them—is to improve your ability to listen with your emotions. The more they feel that you listen to them—that you truly hear them—the more they can develop a greater sense of value and security, for you are continually reminding them that they are important enough to listen to.

How Well Do You Listen?

As in loving, listening can always be improved upon. Your feelings can be the focal point in hearing what your children are really saying. At the same time, you still need to balance what you are hearing with your wisdom, your logic, your intuition, your gut feelings, and your love. Yet, even if you know you are doing all of these things, how do you really know how well you are listening?

One way is to ask yourself, "How good a listener am I?" Then honestly answer the following questions that focus on your listening. After you have done that, have the people you listen to (your children, spouse, siblings, friends) answer the same questions about you. You will find out how good a listener you are. You will also see how accurately you perceive your own listening skills.

Here are the questions.

- ❏ Do you pay attention to what you are feeling while others are speaking, using your feelings to sense what they are really saying?
- ❏ Are you listening to understand your children's needs, or in terms of your own needs?
- ❏ Do you often do something else while you are listening, like reading the paper, watching TV, busying yourself with some sort of work like folding clothes or cooking?
- ❏ Do you finish your children's sentences for them?
- ❏ Are you waiting for others to finish talking so you can respond, rather than listening with your full attention?
- ❏ Do you become impatient if your children are not clear about what they are saying?

❏ Are you frequently too busy to take whatever time it takes to listen to your children?

❏ How often are you more interested in telling your children your point of view than listening to their point of view?

❏ Do you listen more from your logical side or your emotional side?

❏ How often do you hear the hurt beneath the anger in your children?

❏ How often do you interrupt others?

❏ How comfortable are you when listening to others' emotions?

❏ Do you usually respond intellectually when others talk to you about their emotions?

❏ How often does your mind wander when you listen to your children?

❏ How often do you control the conversation, even when your children are talking?

❏ How well do you listen when you are tired?

❏ How well do you listen when someone is upset at you?

❏ Do your children often repeat themselves when talking to you?

❏ How well do you listen when others are talking to you about your faults?

Answering these questions, and then hearing how others answer them about you, will give you a good idea as to how well you listen. You may not always feel comfortable with how others see you as a listener; but if you want to be a good listener, you need to know if the people you are listening to feel like you hear them.

Look at your answers. Listen to others' feedback. What do you see? What can you do more of—less of? What can you improve upon? Do you need to hear someone's needs? Do you need to be more vulnerable with your feelings when you listen? Are you hurting anyone by not seeing or hearing him or her? These questions, and others, can be guidelines to improving your listening skills.

Children and teens want and need to be heard. Whether you are aware of it or not, your children always know when you are listening—and when you are not. If you look at listening as a way of caring and loving, as a way of understanding, you cannot go wrong. You become someone who is always there, ready to listen, ready to care, ready to give what every child and teen needs—safety, comfort, understanding, acceptance, and love.

Bobby's Story

The book could end here, but there is one final story I would like to share with you.

So much has been said about little league parents and coaches and the pressures they have brought to bear upon very young athletes. Yelling, screaming, humiliating, and belittling are, unfortunately, all common descriptions of what goes on during and after the games. Yet, there are other little league coaches and parents who do not fit these descriptions. They are loving and caring and quite the opposite of what one so often hears about or witnesses.

Here is one example of a caring coach, a not-so-talented boy, and a loving father.

Dick got a call late one night from a friend who told him he was in desperate need of his help.

"Dick," he said. "Can you help me out? A family emergency has come up, and I'm going to have to leave town for a couple of weeks. I'm coaching a little league team, and we have two more games left of the season. They are important games. If we win them both, we go to the playoffs. The kids are so excited, and I'm just sick about not being able to be there for them. You are the only guy I want to ask to take over for me. Can you do it?"

Dick said okay. He had never coached, but he was an avid athlete and understood the game of baseball—he had even played little league himself when he was younger.

On his first day with the team, he sat them all down for a meeting.

"I'll coach you, but only under one condition," he began. "You have to agree to play for fun. Does everyone agree?"

They looked at each other and then said all together, yes!

"Okay, let's begin then." Dick said. "But remember, I'm going to hold you to your word."

As they practiced Dick began to coach the boys, who were aged nine to eleven. Some of them had talent. Others were going to be late bloomers. And with some, it was hard to tell how they might turn out.

One boy, Bobby, stood out to Dick. He seemed younger than he actually was. He was nine, but his body was small for his age. The smallest batting hat the team had was still too big for him—it came so far down on his forehead that he sometimes had trouble seeing under the brim. His uniform was too large for his neck, and his catching hand barely filled the space of his glove. But his size did not stop the other players from accepting him—or caring for him. He loved being part of the team; he always tried his hardest, and he never complained. He was excited about everything—except batting.

Dick worked with Bobby on how to swing the bat and how to watch the ball. He tried to calm his fear that he would always strike out—because he had struck out every time he had ever come to bat. The problem was that he was not yet strong enough to swing the bat fast enough to hit a hard-pitched ball.

Saturday finally came, and the team played their first game. All the parents were there rooting and hoping for a win. Bobby's father sat close to the diamond, just behind the batting screen.

The game was close, but they came through and won. One more win and they were in the playoffs.

They practiced as much as possible for the last game, going over strategy and the basics of hitting and fielding. They were ready.

The day of the final game arrived. The teams were so evenly matched that it could go either way. The score seesawed back and forth, neither team being able to hold on to a solid lead. Then the other team suddenly went ahead by two runs. It was the bottom of the last inning and the team's last chance to score. They had several chances but could not break anything loose, until finally one batter reached first base—but they were only one out away from losing the game. And it was Bobby's turn to bat.

He picked up his bat; then he came over to Dick. "Dick . . ." he began. "I'm going to strike out—I just know it. I'm going to lose the game for us. Someone else should bat."

"Bobby," Dick said. "Remember when we all agreed that we were going to play for fun?"

Bobby stood there, looking down at the ground, his batting hat covering his eyes. "Yes, but—" he started to say.

"How much fun would it be if you didn't even try to get a hit?" Dick asked. "If you strike out, then you do, but at least you tried."

"But I'll lose the game for the team," he said, close to tears.

"But at least you will have tried," Dick answered. Then he turned to the rest of the team and asked them. "We all agreed to have fun—win or lose. How many of you think Bobby should take his turn at bat?"

They looked at each other and then all enthusiastically encouraged him to go to home plate. Bobby just looked at Dick, unable to move.

"You can do it," Dick said. "At worst, you will strike out, but at least you will have tried. Go ahead. We are all behind you."

Bobby walked up to the plate to the cheering of both teams—the opposing team encouraging their pitcher, the home team hoping for a miracle.

He took a huge swing at the first pitch, missing it by a mile, swinging about three seconds after the ball had already passed the plate. After readjusting his batting hat so he could see the pitcher, Bobby flung his bat at the second pitch, swinging so hard he nearly threw himself off balance, and missed again.

The opposing team and their parents were yelling at the top of their lungs, wanting a strikeout. The home team and all of their parents yelled just as loudly, encouraging Bobby. His father sat rigid in the stands, ashen-faced.

Bobby waited, his bat ready. The pitch flew towards him. With his eyes closed, he swung as hard as he could. And he missed.

The opposing team went wild, yelling and cheering. They ran out onto the field, celebrating, jumping up and down. The home team was stunned, silent. It was over.

Bobby was still standing next to the plate, slowly pushing the tip of the bat around in the dirt, head down, tears running down his cheeks. His father, hands clasped tightly in his lap, tears welling up in his eyes, watched silently from the bleachers.

Dick was suddenly in front of Bobby, all six foot, five inches of him, down on one knee.

"Bobby!," he said. "That was great!"

"Great? Oh, Dick," Bobby said. "I knew I would strike out—I knew I would. I lost the game."

"But look at what you did, Bobby," Dick said. "You missed the first pitch by a mile. The second pitch, you only missed by three or four inches. And the third pitch, you only missed it by this much."

Dick held his first finger and thumb about an inch apart.

Bobby looked at Dick's finger and thumb and then at him.

"By only that much?" he asked.

"By only that much . . ." Dick said. "I know if you had just one more swing you would have hit it."

Bobby looked at Dick for several seconds. "You really think so?"

"I really do."

He looked at him for a few seconds longer then turned and ran to his father, who was now standing on the sidelines.

"Dad! Dad! I only missed it by this much!" he yelled, holding his finger and thumb about an inch apart as he ran toward him.

His father, laughing, bent down, gathered him up in his arms, and hugged him tightly.

Bibliography and Suggested Reading

Bradshaw, John. *Healing the Shame That Binds You.* Deerfield Beach, FL: Health Communications, Inc., 1988.

Cameron, Julia. *The Artist's Way.* New York: Jeremy P. Tarcher/Putnam, 1992.

Chopra, Deepak. *Ageless Body, Timeless Mind.* New York: Harmony Books, 1993.

Goleman, Daniel. *Emotional Intelligence.* New York: Bantam Books, 1997.

Lazaris. *The Sacred Journey.* Orlando, FL: NPN Publishing, Inc., 1987, 1988, 1999.

Lazaris. *On Releasing Anger/On Releasing Self-Pity,* audio tape. Orlando, FL: Concept:Synergy. (P.O. Box 691867, Orlando, FL 32869. Conceptsynergy@worldnet.att.net, 1-800-678-2356, (407)876-4973.)

Lazaris. *Healing & Releasing Hurt/The Keys of Happiness,* audio tape. Orlando, FL: Concept: Synergy.

Leman, Kevin. *The Birth Order Book.* New York: Dell Publishing, 1985.

Ornish, Dean. *Love & Survival, 8 Pathways to Intimacy and Health.* New York: HarperCollins, 1998.

Palmer, Helen. *The Enneagram In Love And Work.* San Francisco: Harper San Francisco, 1995.

Riso, Don. *Personality Types.* Boston: Houghton Mifflin Company, 1996.

Siegel, Bernie S. *Peace, Love, and Healing.* New York: Harper Perennial, 1989.

Weil, Andrew. *Spontaneous Healing.* New York: Fawcett Columbine, 1995.

About The Authors

Christopher Andersonn, who has a B.S. in Physical Education and a Secondary Teaching Credential, has worked with over fifteen thousand athletes throughout America, Canada, Europe, and Australia at all levels of competition—scholastic, club, Olympic, world class, and professional. He has also given seminars and spoken individually to thousands of their parents on improving emotional well-being, achieving clearer communication, and increasing personal success. He and his wife Barbara live in San Rafael, California.

If you want to contact him personally, you may write to him at chris@ChristopherAndersonn.com or at 16 Salvador Way, San Rafael, CA 94903.

For further information please visit www.ChristopherAndersonn.com.

Barbara Andersonn, MA, MFCC, became a licensed Marriage, Family, and Child Counselor in 1979. She has counseled children, adolescents, and adults privately and in such settings as child guidance clinics, community mental health clinics, and the Los Angeles Juvenile Probation Department. In 1992 she expanded her practice to include athletes, from professionals to the very young, and their parents.

To order "The Emerald Lagoon" visualization/meditation audio tape, please send $10.00 plus $3.00 shipping to 16 Salvador Way, San Rafael, CA 94903. California residents include 7½% sales tax (75 cents).

Index